RELICARIOS

RELICARIOS

Devotional Miniatures from the Americas

BY MARTHA J. EGAN

PROLOGUE BY TERESA GISBERT

PRINCIPAL PHOTOGRAPHY BY
ANTHONY RICHARDSON AND MICHEL ZABÉ

MUSEUM OF NEW MEXICO PRESS ■ SANTA FE

Manufactured in Milan, Italy.

10 9 8 7 6 5 4 3 2 1

PROJECT EDITOR: Mary Wachs
DESIGN: Linda Seals
TYPOGRAPHY: Set in Erhardt by Wilsted & Taylor
ADDITIONAL PHOTOGRAPHY: Almeida-Suter, Mexico City; Ruth M. Anderson; Christoph Hirtz, Quito, Ecuador; Richard Strauss, Smithsonian Institution, Washington, D.C.; Tony Peres, Santa Barbara, California; Ramón Villegas, Manila, Philippines.
MAPS AND LINE ART: Kathy Chilton
FRONTISPIECE: Mid-nineteenth-century to early twentieth-century Bolivian *relicarios*
PHOTO: Anthony Richardson

Library of Congress Catalog Card Number: 93–78896
ISBN: 0–89013–253–4 (CB); 0–89013–254–2 (PB)

Museum of New Mexico Press
P.O. Box 2087
Santa Fe, New Mexico 87504

CONTENTS

18th-century Ecuadoran *relicario*, carved tagua nut on embroidered, appliqued, and sequin-embellished silk in silver frame 7 × 6 × 1 cm. Obverse: *Virgen Coronada*; reverse (not shown): *Virgen Eucarística*. Collection of the Banco Central del Ecuador, Quito, Ecuador. Photo: CH.

PROLOGUE

In Latin America, the baroque period is typified by its attempts to embrace everything, from the shape of a city to art, theater, fashion, and even personal life-styles. The presence of the baroque in Latin America is so deep that it definitively characterizes society in the seventeenth century and into the eighteenth century as well. In order to understand this period, the great manifestations of the baroque, as well as the minor—from the massive structure of a convent to a tiny *relicario*—must be considered. Martha Egan's *Relicarios: Devotional Miniatures from the Americas* introduces us to an important minor aspect of the baroque represented by devotional art and assists us in better understanding this world deliriously obsessed with the afterlife. Octavio Paz's study of the life of Sor Juana Inés de la Cruz and Serge Gruzinsky's *La Guerre des Images* illustrate this complex society of which we are a product but which we scarcely understand.

The Catholicism of the seventeenth-century Counter-Reformation aspired to be universal, not only in the sense of seeking to extend its influence to the ends of the earth but also in its desire to incorporate the dogmas of the church into a simple set of teachings. To accomplish these aims, the church used the powerful weapon of visual arts that would appeal to everyone and be especially captivating to the illiterate masses. This policy was transmitted to the New World via the triumphant baroque, a style that continued to be associated with medieval forms such as the Gothic vaulting used in Latin American architecture until the seventeenth century and, in painting, the Gothic-inspired technique of applied gold leaf, a feature of the Cusco School. Both currents, the medieval and the baroque, converged in an exacerbated religiósity that fetichized all it touched. The custom of making pilgrimage, whereby the believer seeks direct contact with the image of his devotion, evolved during the medieval era; but to baroque influence is owed the loyal believer's search to establish an intimate and personal relationship between himself and the object of his devotion by means of a representational image. Such a union appears to become more concrete when one can possess a part of the desired object. Indeed, this is the function of a relic. This emotional union between the sacred—personified by God, Christ, the Virgin, and the saints—and the person who aspires to communicate with them has been amply studied by Weisbach, who considers the phenomenon to be inherently baroque. Broader still is the posture of Freedberg, who describes the power of images and all of the shades of meaning implied in the relationship between man and the sacralized inanimate object that has "transferred" power such as that located in relics. Such powers are not only transferred into the inanimate body parts, clothing, or personal effects of the holy person, they are also acquired through simple contact. Such is the case of the ribbons cut to the exact height of the Virgin that have been credited with innumerable miracles. The *relicario*, even if it is void of relics, is nevertheless effective because of its connection with the "true image"—the original painting or sculpture that has inspired the *relicario* image. Often the "contact" between the *relicario* and the image that it represents consists of a blessing that is conferred in the sanctuary or principal temple of the saint or Virgin in question.

It should be mentioned that similar traditions existed in the pre-Hispanic world, as shall be discussed in the following work. In the Andes, however, the only saint with pre-Hispanic antecedents who enters into the world of *relicarios* is the apostle Saint James [Santiago], who is identified with Illapa, the god of lightning for the Incas and for some of the cultures that preceded them.

The *relicarios* that contain an image consist primarily of miniatures painted on shell, wood, or metal that in one way or another reflect folk artists' perceptions of mainstream artistic currents. Nevertheless, it should be noted that many well-known painters, such as the Mexican Juan Correa, painted and signed *relicarios*. This should not be surprising, as the borders between popular art and so-called fine art in Latin America are highly imprecise and, more than imprecise, artificial. The artists of the seventeenth and eighteenth centuries devoted equal skill to sculpting a *retablo* as to carving a box for safekeeping tobacco; the same was true with regard to painters.

In time the *relicarios* were replaced by the *detente*, the term deriving from the verb *detener*, meaning "to stop." *Detente* is an imperative meaning "halt immediately," and it is directed at the devil, the complete phrase being "halt, Satan." Many believe that the devil cannot approach a body or a soul if it is protected by a *detente*, which in reality is a shield or coat of arms. As Martha Egan indicates, *detentes* are related to the *escudos de monja* that were so popular among the Mexican Conceptionist and Jeronymite nuns of the eighteenth century. These *escudos* are large *relicarios* that in the case of the Conceptionists had the image of the Immaculate Conception painted on one side.

In her book, Martha Egan has gathered significant Latin American examples of the *relicario* genre, thereby placing one of the most characteristic expressions of viceregal art within the reach of a wide public. Her book allows us to become acquainted with the minutely detailed art of the *relicario* in all its forms, from Mexico to Peru, an art form that is closely linked to the intimate lives of those who felt a strong bond of affection with their heroes, in this case sainted heroes. Ms. Egan's suggestion of a parallel with similar phenomena of our times such as the devotion of adolescents for rock stars is not frivolous. Without a doubt we are being challenged to look at religious art within the context of the private daily life of the individual. This approach will enable us to better understand Latin American society, a society that is developing and revealing itself through a culture that has been primarily motivated by religious conditioning.

Teresa Gisbert
La Paz, Bolivia

Oil on canvas painting, "The Virgin of the Destitute of Valencia," by Tomás Yepes, dated 1652. This painting of a much-venerated Spanish statue shows period *relicarios* and jewelry, gifts to the Virgin from her devotees. The work is in the Convento de las Descalzas Reales in Madrid. Photo courtesy of the Office of National Patrimony, Madrid.

PREFACE

Over the course of buying and selling Latin American folk art these past two decades, and while rooting through museums and private collections of Latin American art, I invariably found myself drawn to little lockets that contained religious imagery—some crude and homemade, some exquisite and masterfully crafted. These objects were commonly called *relicarios*, even though they often did not contain relics. They were familiar to people knowledgeable about Latin American folk art, but nobody could tell me much about them.

My curiosity about these fascinating objects led me to attempt to find out more about them, and thus the research project that evolved into this book was begun. Although there are numerous works on European reliquaries, information on the small, personal reliquary lockets popular throughout the past five hundred years in Latin America appeared to be limited to a couple of short essays written a half-century ago by Mexican scholars Manuel Romero de Terreros and José Miguel Quintana on the *relicarios* and Agnus Dei lockets of Mexico.

Because Spanish and Latin American books, even recent works, rarely have indexes, bibliographies, or footnotes, it was necessary to pore over more than two hundred works, including period documents, to find the scant information that exists on *relicarios*. The task was greatly facilitated by the assistance of no fewer than fifty leading scholars, museum curators, art dealers, and cognoscenti from the United States, Latin America, the Philippines, and Europe who made suggestions, supplied references, and assisted me in obtaining illustrations for this book. Their expertise was invaluable, and their encouragement and generosity were very gratifying to me.

I am particularly indebted to the following scholars who critiqued my manuscript: Ted Bohr, S.J., art historian and professor, Creighton University, Omaha, Nebraska; Gloria Kay Giffords, art conservator and author, Tucson; Teresa Gisbert and José de Mesa, art historians and authors, La Paz, Bolivia; Marion Oettinger, Curator of Latin American Art at the San Antonio Museum of Art; Donna Pierce, Research Associate of the Museum of New Mexico; and Marilee Schmit, Curator at the Carnegie Museum of Natural History.

Judy Sellars, Librarian at the Museum of International Folk Art (MOIFA) in Santa Fe, helped me to obtain innumerable obscure books through the Inter-Library Loan program. Orlando Romero of the Museum of New Mexico's History Library, Santa Fe, was also very helpful, as were librarians at the College of Santa Fe and the University of New Mexico in Albuquerque. Gloria Giffords also made books from her private library available to me.

Additional assistance was provided by Barbara Mauldin of MOIFA; Pat Altman, UCLA; Richard Ahlborn, the Smithsonian Museum of American History; Fatima Bercht, Director of the Americas Society; María Balderrama, Latin American art historian, New York; María Manzari Cohen, Brooklyn Museum; Nancy Morán de Guerra, Director of Inventories, Municipal Museums of Quito, Ecuador; Priscilla Muller, Director of the Hispanic Society of America; Elizabeth Cuellar, Curator Emeritus, UNAM Museum, Mexico City; Johanna Hecht, Associate Curator, Metropolitan Museum of Art; Marita Martínez del Río de Redo, author of various works on Spanish colonial art, Mexico City; Eugenio Sisto, Director, Franz Mayer Museum, Mexico City; Salvador Rueda, former Director, National Museum of History, Mexico City, and Curators María Ester Ciancas and Bárbara Meyer; Estela Ogazón and Jaled Muyaes, collectors, Mexico City; Keith McElroy, Professor of Art, University of Arizona; Gabrielle Palmer, art historian and author, Santa Fe; Irene Silverblatt, Professor of Sociology, University of Connecticut, Storrs; Teodoro Vidal, folklorist and author, San Juan, Puerto Rico; Jim Griffith, Southwest Folklore Center, Tucson; Ricardo Muratorio, Professor, University of British Columbia, Vancouver; Carlos Duarte, Director, Museum of Colonial Art, Caracas, Venezuela; Gary Vikan, Curator of Byzantine Art, Walters Art Gallery, Baltimore; Father Jaime Yáñez, St.

Anthony's Seminary, El Paso; Esperanza Bunag Gatbonton, author of works on Philippine art history, Manila; Sandy Castro, Curator, Intramuros Foundation, Manila; Mark Santiago, Collections, Arizona Historical Society; Ted Bundy, photo archivist, Arizona State Museum; Ward Allan Minge, New Mexico historian, Corrales, New Mexico; María Concepción García Saiz and Araceli Sánchez Garrido of the Museo de América in Madrid; Ramón Villegas, authority on Philippine jewelry, Manila; Stephen Zwirn, Assistant Curator, Dumbarton Oaks; Victor Lieberman, Reference Assistant, Newberry Library, Chicago; and a host of other scholars, museum personnel, and collectors and friends whom I hope will forgive my oversight in not mentioning them by name.

Pat and Angel Colón, Washington, D.C.; Pete Cecere, Mexico City; Kathy Chilton, Rosario Fiallos, Anthony Richardson, Bernadette Rodríguez Caraveo, Albuquerque; Gale Hoskins, La Paz; Jonathon Williams, Austin; Patricia La Farge, Santa Fe; Luis and Andrea Mejía, Houston; and Las Pachamamas—Pat Cardinale, Lolly Martin, Nancy Sutor—in Santa Fe; and many other friends, family members, and colleagues made invaluable contributions to this book.

I would like to thank the Museum of New Mexico Foundation for its very generous grant that helped make the publication of these beautiful images possible.

Muchas gracias a todos.

Martha J. Egan
Corrales, New Mexico
March 1993

The text on the plaque within the painting reads:

A. Sra Prinsipal con su negra,
    esclava.
Arbol de Granadillas, y su Fruta.
Arbol del Nispero, y su Fruta.
Fruta con nombre de Narangillas.
Palma de Cocos grandes.
Arbol de Coquitos de chile.

Viente Alban, pintor en
Quito a. 1783.

Sra. Principal con su negra esclava ("Important Woman with her Black slave"), oil on canvas painting, signed "Vicente Albán, *pintor en Quito, a 1783*," 80×109 cm. The woman on the right is wearing a gold *relicario*. Museo de America, Madrid.

INTRODUCTION

Since time immemorial, people have worn insignia denoting affiliation with a personage, group, place, or idea. Today, teenagers the world over wear images of rock musicians on the fronts of their T-shirts while their elders wear clothing identifying them with a favorite author, fashion designer, or political figure. The popular art form of T-shirts reflects the importance of these personages in contemporary culture and in our personal lives.

In Latin America, especially during the colonial period, people wore medallions with images of the saints, Christ, or Mary on their chests; these devotional lockets were known as *relicarios*—reliquaries.

"Kunstgeschichte ist Geistesgeschichte," Max Dvorak, a turn-of-the-century Viennese art historian, said—"art history is the history of the human spirit." The colonial period in Latin America was an era of official religion and public piety. Christian themes were predominant and pervasive in artistic expression. Throughout the more than three hundred years of colonial rule, in fact, there was little art produced in the Iberian colonies that was not religious. Even into the twentieth century, Latin American popular art, as well as "fine" art created for the church and wealthy patrons, featured Christian imagery.

The omnipresence of Christian references and symbology in colonial Latin America and the Philippines manifested the very real presence of the saints in the daily lives of the Catholic colonists. Holy images adorned both public and private spaces. Every village, profes-

Oil on canvas painting, *Portrait of La Hermana Francisca Leal y Vidrio*, by Feliz Zárate, Guadalajara, Mexico, 1840. 220 × 119 cm. San Antonio Museum of Art.

sion, festival, day of the year, disease, and cause had its celestial patron, and people proudly displayed their personal religious affiliations by wearing devotional jewelry that reflected their religious values and the piety of the age.

The *relicario* was a small pendant that sometimes contained actual relics of the saints—bits of bone or tooth or a scrap of cloth—but for the most part the reliquary designation was symbolical. In Latin America, *relicarios* were most typically the miniature painting or sculpture of a saint protected behind glass or in a small frame of silver or gold with a ring at the top for suspension from a chain or cord. Often the *relicario* was two-sided, with imagery on both the obverse and reverse. These lockets were worn by the faithful as devotional jewelry either under clothing or openly on one's chest; they were given as keepsakes to family members, travelers, and soldiers going into battle; they were placed around the neck of a favorite image in a church or chapel as a votive offering; they were hung on dormitory walls and bedsteads; and they accompanied nuns in the solace of their cloistered convents. The image of a favorite saint treasured in its *relicario* served to inspire, comfort, and protect the bearer from harm.

The *relicario* was but one type of hagiographic badge that devout people wore in the Spanish and Portuguese colonies. In colonial Mexico, Jeronymite and Conceptionist nuns wore at their necks large, elaborate medallions, known as the *escudos de monjas*, or nuns' coats of arms. These were framed embroideries or paintings on copper that depicted the nuns' favorite saints and aspects of the Virgin and Christ. Another type of badge popular throughout the Americas and the Philippines was the *Agnus Dei*, a medallion containing a wax seal made in Rome from paschal candles. On one side was an embossed image of the Agnus Dei, or "Lamb of God," an icon for Christ; the reverse bore images of saints favored by the pope who commissioned the piece. *Detentes*, small cloth badges with a print of the heart of Christ or another holy image, were also popular devotional items in Latin America, as were scapulars—pairs of cloth squares with religious imagery, one worn on the chest, the other on the back. Both types of cloth badges traditionally were worn by the faithful as amulets for the protection of soldiers and children. They were also hung in the home to safeguard the dwelling and all within. The *detente* refers to the inscription that often accompanies the image: *detente bala* ("stop, bullet") or *detente diablo* ("stop, devil").

The *relicarios* of Latin America and the Philippines were often exquisitely crafted jewels and some of the finest examples of artisanry in both the colonial and independence periods. Many renowned painters, sculptors, and silversmiths made *relicarios*, yet most of the work was produced anonymously, and *relicarios* are rarely mentioned in discussions of Latin American art, in spite of their artistic merits. Romero de Terreros offers an explanation: "These medallions should be valued more as objects of devotion than as works of art (Romero de Terreros 1951, 101)."

Few of these finely worked devotional jewels have survived into present times, in part because they were not considered art objects. To a traditional Catholic whose main interest in a *relicario* is its usefulness in prayer and its presence as a comfort, there is little difference between a Virgin of Guadalupe as reproduced in a cheap print encased in tin and plastic and a centuries-old, hand-painted image on copper in a gold filigree frame. The difference in monetary or artistic worth between the two is obvious, but to a person using such an item for devotional purposes, the two are of equal spiritual value.

It is thus sad, but not surprising, that such a personal possession as a *relicario*, an object that once held profound meaning for the person who received it as a gift or who purchased it, would have been sold by that person or his or her descendants in times of financial need or changing values.

Many fine *relicarios* have survived, however, and have passed from the hands of the devout to the gloved hands of curators in today's museums. For those of us who look to the treasures of people long gone for an understanding of their times and values, *relicarios* present a wealth of information. They manifest the tangible connectedness of a people to ancient beliefs and practices; they convey to us an understanding of the real presence of the saints in people's daily lives and their trust in the supernatural; and they tell us of a bygone era when patient, loving hands would lavish countless hours and infinite skill on the creation of artworks not for reasons of fame or fortune but rather in service to faith and religiously inspired ideals.

18th-century Argentinian *relicario*. Enamel on copper in silver frame. Obverse: *San José con el Niño*; reverse: *Santa Ágata*. Private collection. Photo: AR.

Byzantine pendant reliquary cross in gold and cloisonné enamel. Saloniki (?) 12th–13th century, 9.7 × 6.2 × 1.3 cm. Dumbarton Oaks Collection, Washington, D.C.

RELIQUARY TRADITIONS IN EUROPE

ELICS AND RELIC-BEARING lockets, as well as a host of other religious mementos, have served to inspire and comfort millions of Christians throughout the centuries and continue, though to a lesser degree, to be a part of Catholic and Eastern Orthodox church dogma and practices. The *relicarios* of the Iberian colonies in the New World have their origins in ancient Old World beliefs and customs, especially those associated with the *cult of relics*.

The reverence accorded physical remains of the saints is perhaps one of the more curious aspects of the early Christian religion. Yet the collection of souvenirs from revered persons and the ascription of talismanic properties to these fragments are not solely archaic or Christian practices. Through the ages, many cultures and religions worldwide have had analogous practices and beliefs. A contemporary demonstration of this phenomenon was seen at the interment of Iran's Ayatollah Khomeini, when tens of thousands of mourners fought one another for bits of his shroud. It would appear that the Christian practice of venerating saints' relics is but one example of the universal human need to establish tangible connections to revered figures, real or mythical.

In the ancient Hellenic and Roman worlds, the physical remains of gods and heroes were thought to have magical properties, and possession of such treasures conferred religious and political status upon the owner. Among the Greeks, for example, Athens enjoyed special prestige due to its ownership of the bones of Theseus, and among the Diadochi, the successors of Alexander the Great, the Ptolymites of Egypt were held in special regard because of their hegemony over Alexander's tomb (Weckman 1984, 311).

When the first Christians collected souvenirs and mementos from the martyrs and wore them in capsules about their necks, they were continuing practices common throughout the Mediterranean for centuries. In the pre-Christian era the use of all manner of phylacteries and amulets, including a variety of protective items worn around the neck, was a widespread and deeply ingrained custom. Some of these objects were obtained by pilgrims when they visited sacred shrines throughout the region, much as in later times Christians would return home from the Holy Land bearing sacred mementos of their pilgrimage.

One of the most popular types of pre-Christian amulets was the *bulla*. In use by the Etruscans from the fifth century B.C. onward, this was a hollow pendant in gold or leather that might contain perfume or a charm (Buitron 1979, 67). The term *bulla* also refers to a round leather seal worn around the neck by Etruscan and, later, Roman children to protect them from hexing and harm until they reached adulthood. *Bullae* in gold were the insignia worn by Etruscan royalty and the Roman triumvirate while children of common folk were only permitted to wear *bullae* of leather (Doelger 1975, 255). The use of *bullae* persisted into the Christian era, as evidenced by an A.D. fourth-century bronze bust, housed in the Provincial Museum of Trier, Germany, of a boy wearing a *bulla* around his neck inscribed with a Chi-Rho, the Christian monogram for Christ (Doelger 1979, 256).

Among the Greeks, medallions featuring the head of Medusa were worn as apotropaic, or evil-averting, devices. These medallions were often exquisitely worked in gold, with the image of Medusa in repoussé.

In pre-Christian times, Jews also wore amulets containing sacred material, called "phylacteries" or *tefillin*, to protect them from harm, a practice continued into modern times by Orthodox Jewish men.

In the Christian era, any encapsulated item worn about the neck to protect the wearer from witchcraft or harm was called a "phylactery," a term deriving from *philare*—"to keep"; *teras*—"law" (Braun 1940, 23). Into the fourteenth century, it continued to be the most common designation for any item containing relics (Braun 1940, 24). By the fifteenth century, however, the term "reliquary," which first appeared in French, had replaced "phylactery" as the designation for all manner of items containing relics of the saints and martyrs (Braun 1940, 19). Durandus, though, explains the term "phylactery," as it refers to reliquaries, as deriving from *philare*—"to keep or preserve"; *teron* "an extremity." The extremity referred to would be a finger or a toe, those body parts most commonly preserved as relics (Durandus 1893, 57).

The early church initially opposed the collection of relics from martyrs' corpses. Many of the early Christians considered it highly sacrilegious to actually touch the bodies of the saints (Réau 1955, 394). In Jewish law, contact with a cadaver made a man or woman instantly impure. Yet when Moses led the Jews out of Egypt, he took the bones of the patriarch Joseph with them. Jews revered bones but made no cult of relics (Bentley 1985, 36).

The early church did encourage reverence of saints' bodies as a means of increasing fervor among the faithful. Many miracles were attributed to powers of the body, for example that of Saint Paul, even as yet he lived: "And God wrought special miracles by the hands of Paul: so that from his body were brought unto the sick handkerchiefs or aprons, and the diseases departed from them, and the evil spirits went out of them" (Acts of the Apostles 19:11–12, *The Holy Bible, Authorized King James Version* 1950, 161).

The church fathers encouraged the faithful to preserve and venerate souvenirs of the martyrs and confessors, most commonly oil from the lamps that burned in front of the sarcophagi. The gathering of these "oils of the martyrs" was especially popular with regard to the Syrian martyrs. The collection of such sacred mementos reflected the early Christian concept of the *elogia*, or "blessing"—the conference of heavenly favor on a believer through his performance of an act of Christian piety or his contact with a sanctified memento.

Believers dipped bits of cotton in the oil of these lamps, carrying them in special containers called *encolpia* that they wore around their necks. Early Christians also were known to wear *encolpia* that contained small sponges or cloths dipped in the blood of martyrs. Bits of cloth that came into contact with a saint's body were also popular souvenirs of the saints that the faithful collected and wore around their necks. These "indirect relics," as they would later be called, were

Byzantine pendant reliquary of Saint Demetrius in gold and enamel. Saloniki, 13th century, 2.8 cm in diameter. The cover is hinged at the top and the bottom. Within, a pair of doors leads to a small gold relief of Saint Demetrius lying in his tomb. On the reverse of the locket are standing figures of the martyrs Sergius and Bacchus in enamel. Dumbarton Oaks Collection, Washington, D.C.

known as *brandea* (*New Catholic Encyclopedia, Vol. XII* 1967, 235; Réau 1955, 393). The wearing of actual relics of the saints in *encolpia* appears to date from the fourth century when the collection of relics from the saints' corpses became a widespread practice.

The *encolpium* was a small glass or rock-crystal container suspended around the neck. The vessel could be round, cubic, cylindrical, or cross-shaped. *Encolpia* could also be medallions engraved with sacred writing and imagery. While some were crude and of humble materials, others were more elaborate. Gold *encolpia* that date from the fourth century have been found in a cemetery close to the Vatican. These were small cubes etched with the monogram of Christ together with the alpha and the omega. The use of precious metals for such reliquaries is further attested to by Saint Jerome in the late fourth century and by Prudentius in the early fifth century. Saint Helen herself, according to Rufinus, is said to have worn a piece of the true cross of Christ encased in a silver *encolpium* (Doelger 1975, 106). Saint Niceforo in the eighth century refers to the widespread popularity of *en-colpia* and their ancient roots in his refuting of the arguments of the Iconoclasts (*Enciclopedia Universal Ilustrado* 1923, 599).

In fifth- and sixth-century Byzantium, the term *enkolpion* (from the Greek for *encolpium*) referred to a variety of circular pectorals with a central medallion depicting in repoussé a biblical scene or the portrait of an emperor. Two crosswise loops at the top enabled the medallion to be suspended from a chain or thong and hung around the neck. From the third to the seventh century the *encolpia* usually consisted of a disc of gold sheet with repoussé. Sometimes two such discs were joined together with a space in between for a relic.

By the eleventh and twelfth centuries, the term *encolpium* referred specifically to a small cross worn on a necklace by pilgrims returning to Europe from the Holy Land. Such crosses were made of base metal and featured images of Jesus and Mary. They contained small internal cavities in which relics and mementos from sacred sites could be placed (*Out of the Opulent Past* 1992, 232).

In Byzantium, religious souvenir containers were known as *elogiae*. They were most commonly small stamped plaques, tokens, or flasks containing earth, oil, water, or other common substances made holy through contact with someone or something. The *elogiae* were particularly popular among pilgrims. They were thought to confer a blessing on the wearer and were worn or carried by pilgrims as amulets (Vikan 1982, 10).

The Cult of Relics

In A.D. 313 the Edict of Milan, negotiated by Emperor Constantine with his rival, Licinius, mandated toleration of the Christian religion throughout the Holy Roman Empire. The establishment of the *Pax Cristiani*, following three centuries of intermittent persecution, allowed Christians to practice their religion openly. Soon, pilgrims from all over the Christian world began to travel to the sites made holy by the presence of Christ, Mary, the apostles, and the early martyrs—a custom that continues to this day for fervent Christians. Like travelers everywhere, these pilgrims to the Holy Land returned home with souvenirs and mementos of their pilgrimages: small containers of dirt from the hill of Golgotha, vials of water from the Dead Sea, olive pits from the Garden of Gethsemane, and so forth. The most valued souvenirs, however, were relics. These treasured mementos were carefully guarded in capsules of various types and worn in rings, pendants, and crosses by pilgrims or hung by the bed of a sick person. They served the wearer as amulets and talismans as well as objects of piety, devotion, and affiliation.

In many ways the cult of relics grew with the emergence of the Byzantine empire as a major political and economic force in the Mediterranean. In A.D. 330, Constantine built the city he named for himself not as an imitation of Rome but as a Christian city, with monuments, memorials, and churches dedicated most especially to the Virgin Mary.

Just five years before the founding of Constantinople, the Emperor's mother, Saint Helen, discovered Christ's cross. This discovery led to the widespread dispersal of wood particles (*lignum crucis*) purported to be from the true cross and to the increasing popularity of relics in general. By the fifth century the exhumation, dismembering, and transportation of saints' bodies were accepted practices. Indeed, the collection of relics may have begun as early as the second century when citizens of Smyrna proclaimed their devotion to the relics of their holy bishop, Saint Polycarp, shortly after his martyrdom in A.D. 156–157 (*New Catholic Encyclopedia, Vol. XII* 1967, 234).

Relics were brought to Constantinople, Antioch, and Alexandria from all corners of the Christian world, and for centuries they were a principal export from Byzantium. Such treasures as the (ubiquitous) head of John the Baptist, the Virgin's robe and belt, the Crown of Thorns, Christ's bloody mantle, and countless fragments of the bodies and personal effects from a multitude of saints and martyrs found their way into the churches, sanctuaries, and shrines of Byzantium and subsequently into the cloisters and castles of Western Europe and beyond.

The flowering of monasticism in Byzantium between the end of the third century and the end of the fifth century, together with the thousand-year-long history of the Byzantine empire as an important economic and sociopolitical power, led to the emergence in the sixth century of a distinctive style of art whose influence would be felt far and wide for centuries to come.

Byzantine art, almost exclusively church art, was centered in Constantinople and in the monasteries of the East. Patient arts such as the illumination of manuscripts, icon painting, the working of ivory, enameling, and fine gold- and silversmithing were developed by

Gold *encolpium*, 6.5 cm in diameter. Late 6th-century Constantinople. Dumbarton Oaks Collection, Washington, D.C.

monks. The importance of relics in Eastern religious life and commerce assured reliquaries an important role in Byzantium's famed luxury industries. Byzantine artisans created large, sumptuous reliquaries for churches, sanctuaries, and shrines. Small reliquaries—crosses and medallions bearing images of the saints—were also popular items of personal devotion and export (Veyne 1985, 634).

Alongside such trade goods as icons, silks, brocades, copper and gold work, leather, glass and jewels, furs, and slaves, relics and reliquaries were exported to the West by Jewish, Muslim, and Italian traders. Constantinople sat astride the two most important trade routes of the Middle Ages—the silk route and the spice route—and was one of the Mediterranean's most active ports. By the tenth century, trade had made Constantinople one of the great marketplaces of the world (Veyne 1985, 558).

Although Byzantium did not survive as a political entity into the period when Europeans were conquering the Western hemisphere—Constantinople was sacked by the Crusaders in 1203—its art, culture, and civilization, like those of the Islamic world, were far more sophisticated than were those of any city in Western Europe at the time.

Byzantine influences were particularly absorbed into the art forms evolving in Italy, by the eleventh century a halfway point between the sophisticated but politically doomed East and the poorer and less populated but developing West. In the fifteenth, sixteenth, and seventeenth centuries, Italian-trained artists in turn had a profound influence on artistic expression in the New World, most evidently in the Andes.

Before the twelfth century, relics were somewhat rare in Western Europe, but in the Middle Ages the Crusades and special pilgrimages to the Holy Land for the purpose of opening saints' tombs led to the proliferation of relics in the West. Travel to pilgrimage sites in Western Europe also became popular. The sale of relics of local saints made fortunes for such places as Tours, France (Saint Martin); Compostela, Spain (Saint James); and Bari, Italy (Saint Nicholas; Réau 1955, 402). Later, Lourdes, Fatima, and others became important pilgrimage sites where relics and relic-bearing containers were sold as mementos to pilgrims. Rome became the center for the sale of all manner of religious goods and souvenirs, including relics, as it continues to be today.

Relic collecting was often intemperate and reached indecent proportions. At the burial of Saint Elisabeth of Thuringia, for example, fanatical devotees cut off her hair, her fingernails, and even her nipples as talismans (Réau 1955, 404). By the Middle Ages, relics and indulgences had become major sources of income for the church, with abuses abounding. In the sixteenth century the issue of relics became a bone of contention between Rome and those demanding reforms in the church. In his "Treatise on Relics," published in Geneva in 1543, John Calvin denounced the abuses in the cult of relics.

Authenticity and origins of relics were often called into question. One of the great collections of relics, that assembled by Cardinal Albert of Brandenburg, famous for his commerce in indulgences and relics, was offered for sale at Halle in Saxony and included such "relics" as twigs from the burning bush mentioned in the Old Testament; crystal ampoules containing drops of wine from the Wedding Feast at Cana; a bit of Moses' left ear; two feathers and an egg from the Dove of the Holy Spirit; and the inevitable thorns from Christ's Crown of Thorns along with pieces of the true cross. Despite Luther's railing against the "idols of Halle," the cardinal continued to grow rich from his trade in relics. His was not the only collection to include relics of dubious authenticity. In the treasuries of the churches and convents of Western Europe, one could count no fewer than a dozen heads and sixty fingers of Saint John the Baptist (this in spite of the alleged burning of his corpse by Emperor Julian in the fourth century); seven foreskins from the infant Jesus; fifteen arms of Saint James; thirty bodies of Saint George; and six breasts of Saint Agatha (Réau 1955, 405).

Although the Counter-Reformation signaled the beginning of the end for the cult of relics in the Christian world, vestiges of the custom of collecting, preserving, and venerating relics continued for many centuries among the traditional Catholic populations of Europe, most especially in Spain and, by extension, in her New World colonies.

During the Middle Ages the popularity and abundance of relics led to the emergence of an entire genre of decorative art devoted to containers for relics. Powerful monarchies and the monastic orders, who often competed with one another for power and influence, commissioned elaborate, ostentatious reliquaries. Essential to the fueling of this artistic development was the abundance of relics coming into Europe from Byzantium via the Crusaders and merchants. The most skilled gold- and silversmiths of the period were engaged to construct elaborate capsules and containers for relics. This was a significant departure from the earlier types of reliquaries destined for church use, which were simple arcs, urns, and small coffers.

The royalty and the church commissioned craftsmen to make a variety of reliquaries in gold and silver, richly decorated with precious gems and pearls; small caskets for oath-taking ceremonies upon which one swore one's allegiance or to tell the truth (*juraderas* in Spanish); monstrances of dazzling beauty in which the consecrated host would be displayed; and knights' swords said to be "of virtue" and that because they contained relics were more valuable and more effective as weapons (*Catálogo del Museo del Pueblo Español*, 4). Cameos and intaglios with scenes of ancient Rome often decorated reliquaries in the Middle Ages and were held to be among the most valuable of jewels (Evans 1989, 49).

Much of the fine craftsmanship of the Middle Ages, including that dedicated to the fabrication of reliquaries, was centered in the monasteries. Gold work joined sculpture and the illumination of manuscripts as evolving monastic traditions in medieval Western Europe. The goldsmiths' workshops of the great abbeys occasionally provided training for secular goldsmiths (Evans 1989, 44). In the seventh century, reliquaries and jeweled shrines were among the most dazzling objects created by the great goldsmith monks of the age, who included Saint Eloy (circa 588–660), the patron saint of silversmiths and jewelers in Latin America today. Silver was the most common material used for the construction of ecclesiastical reliquaries. Of the 350 listed in the famed treasury of Halle in Saxony, 250 were of silver (Réau 1955, 400).

Reliquary art became one of the most important artistic expressions of the Middle Ages. Whether the reliquary was a large relic-bearing container for a cathedral or a small item of devotional jewelry, no material was too precious: leather, ivory, silver, or, in the case of commissions from the richest abbeys and cathedrals and the royal class, gold, pearls, and jewels. In contrast to the small fragments of relics that common people wore around their necks in simple capsules or lockets, many of the relics purchased by churches or wealthy individuals were large—sometimes whole bodies. The containers for them were necessarily capacious in order to accommodate such "significant" relics as heads, arms, or other large fragments of holy remains.

The Cathedral of Conques, for example, a staging post in south-

17th-century Spanish pendant of the Annunciation
in gold, enamel, jewels, and rock crystal, 7.3 × 3.1 cm.
The Metropolitan Museum of Art. Gift of J. Pierpont
Morgan, 1917.

16th-century Spanish pendant of the Crucifixion
in gold, enamel, and pearls. Height: 5.8 cm.
The Metropolitan Museum of Art. Gift of
J. Pierpont Morgan, 1917.

ern France for pilgrims en route to the shrine of Santiago Compostela,
displays to this day its prize reliquary, a life-size container for the
corpse of Sainte Foy, Saint Faith, a young girl martyred in nearby Agen
in the third century. The reliquary, which dates to the tenth century,
is one of the chefs d'oeuvre of French Romanesque art. It consists of
a seated wooden figure wrapped in silver and encrusted with jewels,
cameos, and filigree, with an oversized head and staring enamel eyes,
Byzantine features, and an uncanny presence.

The quantity and styles of reliquaries were limitless, and patrons
spared no expense in commissioning them. During the twelfth and
thirteenth centuries, the ecclesiastical reliquary art form reached
sumptuous dimensions never again attained in later periods (Braun

1940, 590). Some were in the shape either of the cathedral itself or of a tower. Caskets of various types mounted on feet were perhaps the most common reliquary form until the thirteenth century (*Diccionario Hispano-americano* 1887, 353).

Histories of the Middle Ages sometimes mention noteworthy personal reliquaries of the period. In A.D. 603, for example, Pope Gregory the Great made a gift to King Adoaldo of a reliquary in cruciform shape that contained a sliver of the true cross; an elaborate Crucifixion scene in enamel upon gold further decorated the container. In the ninth century, Charlemagne was said to have treasured a small golden ampoule containing relics of the Virgin's hair and the true cross (Bentley 1985, 203), received from an Islamic caliph (Newman 1981, 63). The design of this locket is reminiscent of the traditional episcopal ring with its enormous circular bezel (Evans 1989, 42). The amulet was buried with the Emperor at Aix-la-Chapelle and disinterred with his remains in A.D. 1000 by Otto III; it remained in the treasury of the Reims Cathedral until 1804, when it was loaned to Empress Josephine to wear at her coronation (Evans 1989, 42).

Charlemagne's devotion to relics helped inspire the popularity of building elaborate reliquaries for their safekeeping and display. The Second Council of Nicaea, convened during Charlemagne's lifetime in A.D. 787, made obligatory the placing of relics in the altar of any church at its consecration. Charlemagne ordered the destruction of altars that did not contain relics (Bentley 1985, 214). The emperor was never canonized, but a cult surrounds him as a Christian hero (Coulson 1964, 105). One of his arms is preserved in a reliquary now in the Louvre (Bentley 1985, 209).

One of the most famed and priceless relics of the Middle Ages was the Crown of Thorns, which Saint Louis purchased from Baldwin, the Latin emperor of Constantinople (Evans 1989, 50). Later, in the late thirteenth century, the King of Aragon commissioned a goldsmith to fabricate a very small reliquary pendant to contain a fragment of this famed relic. It was decorated with two large amethysts and scenes of the Passion in translucent colors of enameled gold. It is now in the British Museum (Evans 1989).

In Spain, many reliquaries were made by Moors as well as Jews, particularly in the twelfth and thirteenth centuries (*Enciclopedia Universal Ilustrado* 1923, 532). The Cathedral of Palencia (Castille), for example, boasted a magnificent reliquary of carved ivory made in

17th-century Spanish (or Italian) gold and rock crystal *relicario* with enameling and containing actual relics, 6.2 × 4.5 cm. Hispanic Society of America, New York.

18th-century relic-bearing Spanish *relicarios* in silver frames, 6 × 4.3 × 1 cm; 8 × 6 × 1.5 cm. Private collection. Photo: AR.

Cuenca in A.D. 1050 by an Arab craftsman and given to the church by the father of the last Moorish king of Toledo, Al Hachit Hosano (*Enciclopedia Universal Ilustrado* 1923, 530).

Beginning in the late Middle Ages, the custom of preserving relics so that they could be viewed came into vogue. Pieces of bone, cloth fragments, and other relics were set into sections in a sheet of parchment, card, or wood and covered with crystal or glass. Fine calligraphy, called *filacteria* in Spanish, encircled the aperture and identified the saint whose relics were contained within. Many of these reliquaries were large and very elaborate and formed portions of altar retables.

16th–17th-century Iberian reliquary bust. Polychromed and gilded
wood with jewels and relics behind rock crystal, 58 × 17 × 52 cm.
Private collection. Photo: MZ.

Some were in the forms of busts, arms, heads, or caskets, with covered
sections that afforded views of the relics within and *filacteria*. This
form of reliquary was very popular in Spain and Italy into the nineteenth century, both in churches and private chapels. Although such
items were crafted in many parts of Latin America during the colonial
period, this style of reliquary is more typical of the Old World than of
the New World.

Smaller wall versions of these window reliquaries were fashioned
for homes and private chapels. They in turn inspired a style of locket
reliquaries that could be worn or hung either beside or on the image

of a favorite virgin or saint. Such *relicarios* were typically two-sided, with tiny relics in apertures surrounded by *filacteria* on one side and a painted or printed image on the reverse. Some were small and simple while others were large and ostentatious, decorated with jewels, pearls, and precious metals.

This type of window *relicario* pendant, containing actual relics, was popular for centuries throughout Europe, particularly in Italy, southern Germany, Spain, and Portugal; its use continued into this century. Such *relicarios* were also treasured and worn by Catholics throughout the New World and the Philippines. In some cases, these lockets were accompanied by a certificate of authenticity issued by an ecclesiastical authority written in Latin. These documents are called *auténticas* in Spanish.

Capsule reliquaries such as these, intended for personal devotion, were privately commissioned and not made for church use. They came to be church property, however, through gifts and wills (Braun 1940, 294). These wearable *relicarios* were often given to the favorite image of a virgin or saint in the church as votive offerings.

Another popular means of wearing actual relics was the reliquary cross, a wooden or metal cross with small windows displaying relics that were identified in calligraphy. Like the lockets, these crosses had a ring at the top that enabled them to be suspended and hung around the neck. Many of these crosses contained a *lignum crucis*, a fragment of the true cross. In Spain, reliquary crosses in slate from Santa María de Nieva and reproductions of the reliquary of Caravaca were particularly prized (*Catálogo del Museo del Pueblo Español*, 8).

In the late Middle Ages, reliquary rings became popular forms of devotional jewelry. Hernán Cortés is said to have worn such a jewel during his campaign to conquer Mexico. The ring contained a large diamond and a medallion in the cap. It is still preserved in Mexico in its leather case (Barba de Piña Chan 1960, 49).

By the late sixteenth century in Europe, the golden age of large ecclesiastical reliquaries was over. Likewise, reliquaries for wearing, a fashion that had reached the height of popularity during the Middle Ages, declined in both quality and favor in Western Europe. Some exquisite devotional jewelry, however, was made during the Renaissance and into the eighteenth century by Europe's leading artisans, especially in Spain (see Priscilla E. Muller's *Jewelry in Spain 1500–1800*, 1972).

Spanish arm reliquaries. Second half of the 18th century. Polychromed and gilded wood with relics behind rock crystal. Private collection. Photo: MZ.

Although the Age of Reason and the secularization of society rendered public display of religious affiliation unfashionable, many types of devotional jewelry, including *relicarios*, continued to be worn by devout women in the conservative regions of Catholic Europe into the twentieth century. This was especially true in certain regions of Spain and Portugal, where *relicarios* and other types of religious jewelry long remained part of traditional regional dress.

Among all the regions of Spain, the western province of Salamanca has best preserved its traditional costume, specifically in Segovia, Salamanca, La Alberca, Montehermoso, and Lagartera. In 1917 Ortiz Echagüe described the women's festival dress of La Alberca, the *traje de vistas*, that included elaborate necklaces of which *relicarios* were an integral part: "Covering the bodice a silk kerchief, and on top of that, as jewelry, strands of seed pearls, enormous necklaces of fine filigreed silver and gold with red corals. From these are hung medals, rosaries, figures of Christ, amulets, commemorative medallions, *relicarios* (Ortiz Echagüe 1917, 28)." The central part of this heavily adorned necklace, worn especially for weddings, was called the *vuelta grande*, the large loop; finer chains called *brazaleras*, which included numerous *relicarios*, medallions, and other ornaments, were fastened to each side of the woman's bodice at the shoulders.

Woman of La Alberca,
Salamanca, Spain, 1929,
wearing the *vuelta grande*,
"large loop" necklace featuring
medallions, *relicarios*, and
miscellaneous silver, glass, and
jet ornaments. Hanging from
her shoulders are *brazaleras*,
silver chains with *relicarios* and
other pendants. Hispanic
Society of America, New York.
Photo: RMA.

Brazaleras from a woman's
festival costume, La Alberca,
Salamanca, Spain, featuring
19th- and 20th-century
relicarios and silver medallions.
Hispanic Society of America,
New York. Photo: RMA,
c. 1929.

Although these necklaces prominently feature Catholic devotional objects such as crucifixes and *relicarios*, it is thought that they are of Arab origins, and their use dates from as early as the thirteenth century (Ortiz Echagüe 1917, 28).

A nineteenth-century French account mentions *relicarios* as being part of the traditional dress in Valencia as well: "Her neck is adorned with a silver or gold chain [*cadena del cuello*] from which a cross or reliquary has been suspended (Williams 1908, 118)." Festival dress of the region included more elaborate *relicarios*: "A reliquary/*relicario* in a small silver medallion is hung around her neck; also a very delicate rosary necklace/*rosario* in gilded silver (Williams 1908, 118)."

Although skilled artisans often created fine, unique *relicarios* for their clients, in Spain the most common *relicarios* were souvenirs from Rome, the Holy Land, or other pilgrimage sites, as well as inexpensive trade items sold in markets, fairs, religious-goods shops, and by itinerant peddlers. These *relicarios* were commonly made of brass and featured cheap colored religious prints and sometimes minuscule relics with tiny strips of paper identifying the saint to whom the relics belonged. Church-issued certificates of authenticity often were included.

The large collection of Spanish folk jewelry in the Museo del Pueblo Español in Madrid features *relicarios* from the sixteenth through the nineteenth centuries and affords the opportunity to examine the characteristics of a wide variety of popular or common Spanish *relicarios*. The Museum of Decorative Arts in Madrid also has a large collection of these popular jewels.

Among Spanish *relicarios* of the past two hundred years, silver casings are most common, including some of low-grade silver, but gilded or silvered copper bezels are not unusual. All manner of silversmithing techniques were employed in the fabrication of *relicario* frames: casting, chasing, filigree, enameling, repoussé, engraving, and stamping. The stones were invariably paste, and some *relicarios* were decorated with coral, shell, and bone.

Silversmiths also created other types of wearable containers in the *relicario* mode: tiny caskets, filigree boxes and jars, small book-shaped containers, diminutive retables, miniature chapels, spheres, and pouches in the shape of flowers or hearts.

The most numerous *relicarios* in the Museo del Pueblo Español's collection are lockets that contain small painted or bas-relief images behind crystal in frames or bezels with a ring at the top for suspension. By the nineteenth century in Spain, the concept of *relicario* included a wide variety of lockets, not solely those encapsulating actual relics. The term gradually came to refer to lockets containing any item of personal adornment that had some religious reference: a small painting on copper, silver, tin, parchment, wood, paper, or glass (including reverse paintings); a print, embroidery, or engraving of a religious scene or holy personages; a small enamel; and a miniature sculpture in ivory, wood, alabaster, lead, or other material.

These, too, come in a variety of shapes: rectangular, oval, heart-shaped, and octagonal. Although these miniature paintings are rarely signed, some are finely painted and surely the work of professional artists. Others are the work of folk artists and display a characteristic simplicity and charm. Many of these *relicarios* also contain hand-colored woodcuts or engravings. The miniatures in this class of *relicario* represent a variety of techniques: wax reliefs, bone carvings, engraved or enameled metal plaques, stamped medals, embroideries, and tiny figures dressed in silks. The variety of frames encasing these works is vast. Some frames are unique and exquisitely worked while others are mass-produced in inexpensive metals. In nineteenth-century Spain and in the New World, it was popular to include tiny cloth or paper flowers in the frames of portraits, as well as bits of ribbon and cord.

Eventually the term *relicario* came to be used colloquially to describe secular as well as devotional lockets, medallions that encased mementos or "relics" of loved ones—a portrait, a lock of hair, a letter, a pressed flower, or a bit of clothing.

The *relicario* was a part of Spain's folk customs for centuries. At the turn of the century, the following *seguidilla*-style Spanish air became popular and was immortalized in Sarita Montiel's 1957 film, *El Último Cuple* (*The Last Couplet*). *El Relicario* remains a favorite in the classical Spanish guitar repertoire:

El Relicario

> *Un día de San Eugenio yendo hacia el Prado le conocí.*
> *Era el torero de más tronío, el más castizo de to' Madrid.*
> *Iba en caleza pidiendo guerra y yo al mirarlo me estremecí.*
> *Y él al notarlo saltó del coche y muy garboso vino hacia mí.*
> *Tiró la capa con gesto altivo, y descubriéndose me dijo así:*

> *Pisa morena, pisa con garbo.*
> *Que un relicario, que un relicario me voy a hacer*
> *Con el trocito de mi capote*
> *Que haya pisado, que haya pisado*
> *Tan lindo pie.*

> *Un lunes abrileño en que él toreaba yo a verle fui.*
> *Nunca lo hiciera que aquella tarde de sentimiento creí morir.*
> *Al dar un lancé cayó en la arena, se sintió herido, miró hacia mí*
> *Y un relicario sacó del pecho que yo enseguida reconocí.*
> *Cuando el torero caía inerte en su delirio decía así:*

> *Pisa morena, pisa con garbo.*
> *Que un relicario, que un relicario me voy a hacer*
> *Con el trocito de mi capote*
> *Que haya pisado, que haya pisado*
> *Tan lindo pie.*

> One Saint Eugene's Day I was on my way to the Prado
> When I saw him for the first time,
> The most swaggering and classiest bullfighter in all Madrid.
> He was in his carriage out carousing;
> And when I looked at him a shudder ran down my spine.
> And he, when he saw his effect on me,
> Stepped down from his coach and strode gallantly to where I stood.
> He swept off his cape with an arrogant toss,
> Spread it out at my feet and said to me—

Chorus

> Dance on this, my brown beauty, dance on this with flare.

19th-century Spanish *relicario*: *Santa Teresa* (obverse). Oil on glass in silver filigree frame, 8.5 × 7.5 × .5 cm. Private collection. Photo: AR.

For a *relicario*, a *relicario* I shall make for myself
To hold the scrap of my cape
That has been danced on and pranced upon
By such a lovely foot as thine.

It was a Monday in April when he was fighting the bulls,
And I went to see him fight,
Never dreaming that on that very afternoon
I would nearly perish from grief.
For on making his pass at the bull he fell to the sand;
Knowing he was wounded he looked up at me.
And he took from his breast a *relicario*
That in an instant I recognized.
And as the bullfighter was breathing his last
In his delirium he cried out to me—

Chorus

Dance on this, my brown beauty, dance on it with flare;
For a *relicario*, a *relicario* I shall make for myself
To hold the scrap of my cape
That has been danced upon and pranced upon
By such a lovely foot as thine.

(trans. M. Egan)

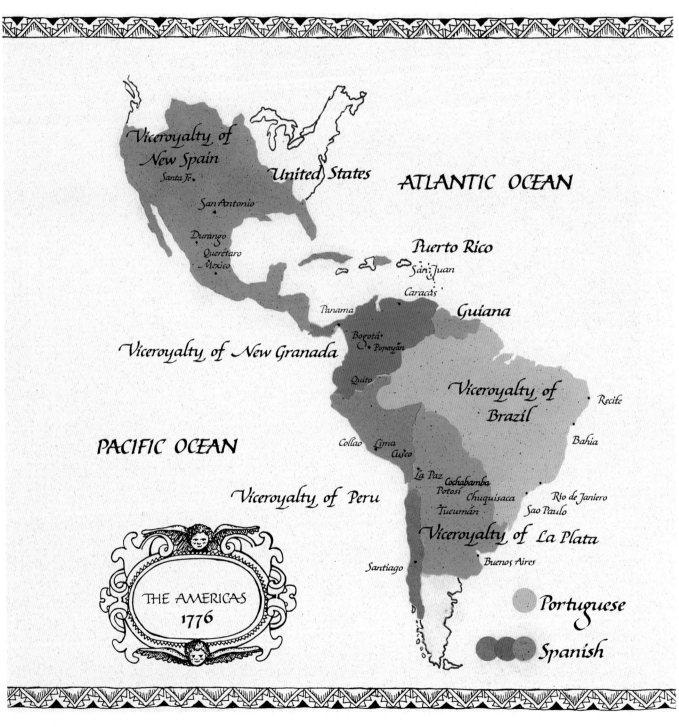

Viceroyalty of
New Spain

Santa Fe

San Antonio

Durango
Querétaro
Mexico

United States

ATLANTIC OCEAN

Puerto Rico
San Juan

Caracas

Panama

Guiana

Viceroyalty of New Granada

Bogotá
Popayán

Quito

Viceroyalty of
Brazil

Recife

PACIFIC OCEAN

Collao Lima
Cusco

Bahia

La Paz Cochabamba
Potosí
Tucumán

Chuquisaca

Río de Janiero
Sao Paulo

Viceroyalty of Peru

Viceroyalty of La Plata

Santiago

Buenos Aires

THE AMERICAS
1776

Portuguese

Spanish

2 THE CULT OF RELICS IN THE NEW WORLD

HEN THE SPANISH AND POR-tuguese set forth to conquer the New World for God, country, fame, and fortune, they carried a variety of small personal devotional items to inspire and comfort them: crucifixes, rosaries, breviaries, medals, images of the saints, holy relics, and *relicarios*. The abundance of these goods among the generally meager possessions of Iberian settlers reflects both the importance of devotional items to their owners and the piety of the age.

Reliquary jewelry was but one vestige of medieval culture that traveled to the New World with the conservative, rural population that made up the majority of sixteenth- and seventeenth-century Iberian immigrants. The medieval cult of relics, affected little by the urbane worldliness of the Renaissance in the nether regions of Spain and Portugal, continued to be an integral part of the Catholic doctrine and practices in the colonies.

Dating from the earliest voyages to the New World, relics were part of the trade goods, church supplies, and personal possessions of passengers aboard Spain's ships. Fragments of iron-framed *relicarios*, complete with the *filacteria* that once identified the relics contained within, were found along the Río de la Plata in present-day Argentina in one of the oldest European sites in the region, one that may date to the first quarter of the sixteenth century (Onelli 1916, 15).

Relicario de San Pedro y San Pablo, 1579–1580, unknown artisan, Mexico. Gilded silver with emeralds and relics said to be from Saint Peter and Saint Paul, 47 × 15 × 12 cm. Museo Nacional del Virreinato, INAH, Tepotzotlán, Mexico. Photo: A-S.

Relics are frequently mentioned in accounts of perilous sea voyages to the New World. In 1555, for example, an English traveler, Robert Thompson, saw friars cast relics into the sea in an effort to calm a storm when bad weather imperiled their Spanish ship off the coast of Veracruz (Weckman 1984, 317).

In his *Compendio y Descripción de las Indias Occidentales*, the Carmelite Antonio de Vásquez de Espinosa relates how the inhabitants of Arequipa in the southern highlands of Peru turned to treasured relics for solace when a nearby volcano erupted in the seventeenth century: "The darkness was great and a tremendous quantity of ash rained down. On that day a solemn and devout procession left the *Compañía* [the Jesuit Church], with twelve priests carrying twelve reliquaries with significant relics, and saints' bones (Vásquez de Espinosa 1969, 472)."

Relics of Christ, the Virgin, and the saints were venerated and treasured in the New World (Weckman 1984, 312). They also sometimes served as trade goods and gifts. When the English Dominican Thomas Gage and his party left San Juan de Ulloa on their journey to Mexico City in 1625, they thanked their Indian hosts in the following manner: "And thus we took our leaves, giving unto the chief of them some beads, some medals, some crosses of brass, some *Agnus Dei*, some reliques brought from Spain, and to every one of the town an indulgence of forty years (Gage 1648, 25)."

The quantity and variety of relics are legion in the Viceroyalty of New Spain, as well as throughout the Iberian colonies in the Americas and the Orient. As in medieval Europe, relics were valued by all and constituted prize possessions in the New World. Church factions, the clergy, churches, and monasteries vied with one another for the prestige of owning noteworthy relics.

From the earliest days of *la colonia*, skilled and trained silversmiths—Europeans as well as native born—made *relicarios* in the Americas. The scarcity of large ecclesiastical *relicarios* in church inventories, however, indicates that this form was not as popular in the colonies as it had been in Spain. Only a small number have survived into modern times.

During the colonial period in the New World, two basic types of relics were venerated: those that were brought to the Americas from Europe and those that were the remains of or personal objects belonging to missionaries, nuns, or holy persons who died in the Americas *en olor de santidad*, in the odor of sanctity. The rigors of life in the colonies and the religiosity of the age produced American saints soon after the Conquest.

One of the most popular American saints was a Spanish Franciscan monk, San Francisco Solano, who died in Lima in 1610. Fray Diego de Córdova, a colleague of the venerable monk, described the miraculous properties of the holy monk's relics: "The intercession of this apostolic man, his merits, his relics, the earth of his burial place, the oil of the lamps in his tombs, calm the elements when there are storms at sea; they have the virtue of being able to quench fire, cheer the sorrowful, grant success in childbearing, heal the palsied, aid those with abcesses, or bleeding; they give sight to the blind, hearing to the deaf, health to the cripples and life to the dead (De Córdova Salinas 1957, 539)." The burials of San Francisco Solano were indeed plural, as his corpse was exhumed numerous times for the purpose of collecting relics. During one of these disinterments, an Augustinian allegedly bent over the corpse as if to kiss it but instead bit off a finger and carried it away in his mouth. This precious relic is later said to have effected miracles (De Córdova Salinas 1957, 825).

A diminutive gold *relicario* containing an ivory carving of San Francisco Solano was found along the Florida coast in 1981. It is believed to have come from the Spanish ship the *Santo Cristo de Román*, part of the Spanish fleet sunk in 1715. The reverse of the arcade-form *relicario* was engraved "*Sn fra-co solano*."

In New Spain, the relics of such New World saints as the Venerable Gregorio López, Fray Pedro Galarza (1535–1611), Madre María de Jesús (b. 1582), and the Jesuits Pedro Rodríguez (Oaxaca, d. ca. 1575) and Juan de la Plaza (d. 1629) were venerated from the moment of death. Not only their remains but the clothing and personal effects of these holy personages were treasured and thought to have miraculous properties. The habit in which the Dominican nun Santa Rosa de Lima (1586–1617) was buried was changed various times following her death for the purpose of collecting relics (López 1993). The faithful also gathered dirt from her tomb, which they mixed with water and drank as a curative (López 1993). In the early colonial period it was also customary to keep as holy relics the fingers with which a holy friar had blessed the faithful (Weckman 1984, 312).

There is little information on how the native peoples of the Americas viewed the Catholic Europeans' veneration of relics. In at

16th-century principal altar retable containing thirty reliquaries. Commissioned by Don Rodrigo de Salazar. Chapel of Santa Marta, San Francisco Church, Quito, Ecuador. Photo: CH.

16th-century polychromed and gilded wood-bust reliquary. Detail of the altar retable of the Chapel of Santa Marta, San Francisco Church, Quito, Ecuador. Photo: CH.

16th-century gold and ivory *relicario*, 3 cm high. The reverse is engraved *Sⁿ, fra^co, solano* ("San Francisco Solano"), born 1549 Andalusia, Spain, died 1610 Lima, Peru. The arcade-form pendant is believed to be from the wreck of the *Santo Cristo de San Román*, part of the Spanish fleet sunk in 1715 off the coast of Florida. Photo courtesy of Christie's.

least certain parts of the Andes this practice was not entirely alien to the indigenous people. Various groups throughout Peru had the custom of mummifying important personages and revering their remains. In pre-Columbian Cusco, for example, during the summer solstice celebration of Inti Raymi, the mummified corpses of the Incas would be taken out of storage and put on view for the people of the realm. When the Inca Huayna Capac died in Quito in 1523, shortly before the arrival of the Spanish, his body was embalmed and carried to Cusco, where it joined the mummified remains of previous Incas in the Temple of the Sun. The heart and internal organs were buried in Huayna Capac's beloved Quito (Vásquez de Espinosa 1969, 544).

In 1625 the Augustinian Fray Baltazar Salas described the veneration of Incan relics on the sacred island of Coati in Lake Titicaca, just off the coast from the present-day pilgrimage site of Copacabana: "There a coffin or stone box was kept, and another of tin that contained a silver tube with a female forearm that had been mummified in the manner of the Egyptian peoples, and accompanying it were various amulets, *kipus* [knotted strings used by Inca nobles for accounting and communication] and coins of gold and silver. It is, they say, the tip of the arm of the first Queen and the mother of the Incas, Mama Ojgllo Huacu; it was brought here by her son Sinchi Roca (Sanjinés 1909, 46)."

Father Bernabé Cobo, who left us much information on Incan religious customs, describes another native Peruvian custom that must have seemed somewhat familiar to the European friar: "Although Paullu-Inca died a Christian and as such he was buried inside the Church, in spite of that, the Indians made for him a small statue and they put inside it some fingernails and hair that they had secretly taken from him; that statue became as venerated by them as the other corpses of the Inca Kings (Cobo 1990, 103)."

In New Spain a primary use for the relics was in the altar stones that, until Vatican II, canon law required churches to have for the celebration of mass. These stones were slabs that covered the top of the altar table; within was a small sealed cavity that contained relics of early Christian martyrs. In A.D. 787 the Second Council of Nicaea made obligatory the placing of relics under the altar of any church at its consecration (Bentley 1985, 214). In his inventories of the Franciscan mission churches of New Mexico in 1776, Fray Atanasio Domínguez invariably mentions their altar stones, gifts to the missions from the king (Domínguez 1956, 351). In 1709, a cargo of an estimated thirty tons of religious objects, including fragments of bones labeled with the names of saints, was pirated off the coast of Guayaquil (Ecuador) by a legally commissioned English privateer, Woodes Rogers. These relics were reportedly destined for use in reliquaries and altar stones of the new churches in the Viceroyalty of Peru (Keleman 1969, 335).

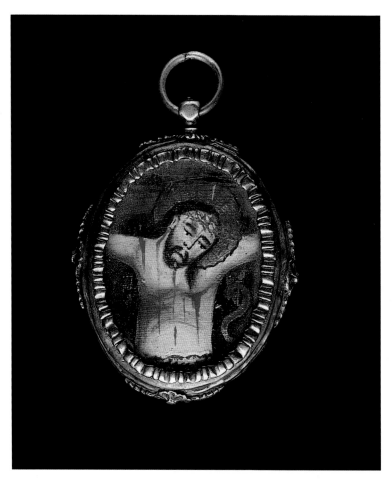

18th–19th-century Mexican *relicario*. Watercolor
on card in silver frame, 7.5 × 5.1 cm. Collected
by Donald and Dorothy Cordry about 1947 in
Oaxaca, Mexico. Obverse: Christ crucified;
reverse (not shown): a piece of cloth with metallic
braid, metal discs, two paper horseshoes with
writing on them, and other sewn-on items.
Museum of International Folk Art, Santa Fe,
New Mexico. Photo: AR.

3
RELICARIOS IN THE VICEROYALTY OF NEW SPAIN

OR THE FIRST TWO HUNDRED years of Spanish rule there were only two political divisions in the Americas. The Viceroyalty of New Spain, established in 1535, covered a vast expanse of territory that included present-day Mexico, Central America, and portions of the southwestern United States, the Caribbean, Venezuela, and, after 1570, the Philippines. The Viceroyalty of Peru, established in 1542, encompassed all of what are now the Spanish-speaking countries of South America. In 1717 the Viceroyalty of New Granada was created for the separate government of present-day Colombia, Venezuela, Ecuador, and Panama. In 1776, the territory now divided into the countries of Bolivia, Paraguay, Uruguay, and Argentina came under the authority of the Viceroyalty of the Río de la Plata.

For two decades prior to Cortés's conquest of Mexico, the Spanish had established colonies in the outer Caribbean. There the native populations were simple hunter-and-gatherer societies, most of which quickly perished from European diseases, warfare, and mistreatment. In Mesoamerica, however, the Spanish encountered a highly sophisticated and well-organized militaristic theocracy that reigned over a population of artisans, farmers, traders, clerics, clerks, teachers, scientists, intellectuals, healers, politicians, and others. The Aztecs and their subject peoples presented much more of a challenge to Spanish rule and culture than had the Caribs and Arawaks of the outer Caribbean. In Mesoamerica the Spanish were also afforded greater opportunities for riches. As the conquerors soon discovered, there was a huge wealth of gold in Mexico and people skilled at working precious metals.

Even as the Spaniards were still in the process of consolidating their power over the Aztec realm, Cortés requested that the Aztec ruler Moctezuma have his artisans craft some Spanish-style religious goods as a test of the skills of these native craftsmen: "And he ordered them to make in gold such things as holy images, crucifixes, medals, jewelry and necklaces, and many other of our things and they did it as perfectly as we could explain these things to them (Cortés 1988, 61)."

Although the Spanish destroyed and smelted most of the beautifully fabricated gold objects either given to them by the Indians or stolen from them, the conquerors could not fail to be impressed by the skills of native craftsmen. They quickly had these artisans working gold for them. Various chroniclers of the early colonial period mention the work of the native goldsmiths and imply, as does Bernal Díaz del Castillo, Cortés's chronicler, that they were taught new techniques by the Spaniards. Díaz del Castillo, who finished his account of the conquest of Mexico in 1568, describes the working of precious metals by native craftsmen in the period following the Conquest: "We shall proceed and relate how all the Indians native to these lands have learned well indeed all the occupations that there are among us in Castille and the smiths of gold and silver, those who hammer as well as cast, are very consummate artisans (Díaz del Castillo 1955, 581)."

Díaz del Castillo goes on to describe the high level of skill exhibited by these native artisans: "In my judgment neither such a renowned painter as the ancient Apelles, nor the ones of our times known as Berruguete and Michelangelo . . . can create with their brushes works of ground pigments or *relicarios* such as those made by three Indian masters of that craft, Mexicans, who are known as Andrés de Aquino, Juan de la Cruz, and Crespillo (Díaz del Castillo 1955, 581)."

From the earliest days of colonial rule, the Spanish Crown sought to exert strict control over nearly all aspects of life and commerce in her colonies. Royal edicts attempted to regulate such minutia as the thickness of colonists' shoe soles and hat decorations. The Crown also attempted to regulate the sale of certain worked objects and to confine such commerce to certain streets to facilitate the collection of taxes.

This included the sale of devotional items. One such regulation stated: "It is hereby decreed and ordered, that *relicarios*, crosses, adornments and trifles of that sort, with filigree or without it, shall not be made, traded or sold by persons other than silversmiths and *relicarieros* [*relicario* makers] or filigree makers belonging to their factory." This law made an exception for religious communities, however, who were allowed to freely trade in such items (De Valle Arizpe 1961, 145).

In addition to regulations governing trade and commerce, the Crown, influenced by the asceticism of the Counter-Reformation and always on the verge of bankruptcy, made laws that attempted to curtail the colonists' predilection for luxury goods; these came to be known as the Sumptuary Laws. Gil González Dávila, the conqueror of Nicaragua, held that the numerous laws forbidding the working of silver and gold were necessary "to prevent the infinite ambition of women and the damages caused by excessive and harmful expenditures (De Valle Arizpe 1961, 98)." Crown edicts against the ostentatious display of wealth often exempted religious jewelry: "the *agnus dei* in gold or silver may be worn by whomsoever without violating the aforesaid edict (De Valle Arizpe 1961, 361)."

Hernán Cortés himself wore religious jewelry, including medals and *relicarios*. Bernal Díaz del Castillo describes Cortés as wearing what could be either a struck medal or a *relicario*: "He wore a small gold chain, beautifully crafted, with a jewel that bore the image of Our Lady the Holy Virgin Mary, with her precious Son in her arms, with a legend in Latin that said that it was Our Lady, and on the other side of the jewel was the image of Saint John the Baptist, with another legend (Díaz del Castillo 1955, 557)."

The wearing of jewelry that was religious in nature was one of the ways in which the women of the Spanish colonies evaded royal edicts forbidding luxuries: "They all had beautiful *relicarios* and fine jeweled rosaries, often with an Agnus Dei, gold embroidered and pearl embellished by the nuns in the convents (Davis and Peck 1963, 52)."

Even in such outposts as far-off New Mexico, women of the Spanish colonies wore and treasured their religious jewelry as precious heirlooms. The 1762 will of Juana Luján, a prominent landholding New Mexican woman from Santa Cruz, near present-day Española, lists various *relicarios*. To her daughter Luisa, she willed "a necklace of pearls mixed with corals and its *relicario* in the center (Ahlborn 1990, 348)," as well as "three silver *relicarios* and one with a wax Agnus

18th–19th-century brass *relicario* of Spanish or Mexican origin, with painting of Saint Ursula in watercolor on card, 7.4 × 4.5 cm. Ward Minge Collection, Corrales, New Mexico. Photo: AR.

18th–19th-century silver *relicario* with religious mementos. Probably of Mexican origin. New Mexican family heirloom. Ward Minge Collection, Corrales, New Mexico. Photo: AR.

(Ahlborn 1990, 352)." To the widow of her son Francisco Gómez del Castillo, Doña Juana left another *relicario* (Ahlborn 1990, 334).

It was a common practice among devout colonial women to give jewelry, including *relicarios* and *Agnus Dei* lockets, to a favorite image of the Virgin or a saint. Numerous wills confirm this practice, as do paintings showing images of the saints and virgins hung with reliquaries, rosaries, and other votive offerings. Documents listing the inventories of churches sometimes specify the jewel or jewels that were gifted to an image by a specific donor.

In his 1776 report on the missions of New Mexico, Fray Atanasio Domínguez mentions *relicarios* as belonging to images in many of the mission churches throughout New Mexico. At the Cathedral of St. Francis in Santa Fe, the image of Nuestra Señora del Rosario was hung with "nine silver gilt *relicarios* and fourteen plain silver ones (Domínguez 1956, 26)."

At Taos, Domínguez not only describes *relicarios*, he also tells a story that suggests why most of them disappeared from church treasuries. Domínguez relates how Father Olaeta, shortly after his arrival in Taos, informed the *alcalde mayor*, his lieutenant, and the principal Indian men of the pueblo that he wished to convert the silver offerings, including some ten *relicarios* that had accumulated on the statue of Our Lady, into a small silver ciborium and cruets for her altar. Father Olaeta then wrote to his superiors in Chihuahua asking their permission to proceed and subsequently shipped the silver medals, crosses, and *relicarios* to Chihuahua. In a letter to Father Olaeta dated 4 February 1776, Don Pedro Velarde, his superior, replied: "The little vessel and cruets which your Paternity has ordered have not been made, and the silver destined for that purpose, which consists of frames of reliquaries and other things of that kind, is, indeed, here in a *chacual* [a leather basket] with a memorandum that they belong to your Paternity (Domínguez 1956, 106)."

These and other church documents indicate that in spite of the relative poverty of the northern missions of New Spain, the colonists did possess *relicarios*, they were treasured as heirlooms, and they were often given to statues of the Virgin as votive offerings.

In New Spain, as elsewhere in the Spanish colonies, *relicarios* were first and foremost the work of metalsmiths. Whether the *relicario* was a mass-produced trinket—a simple base-metal or silver locket encasing a religious print or relic—or an elegant bejeweled pendant en-

18th–19th-century red coral necklace with *relicarios*, *Agnus Dei*, medals, and other religious pendants. Museo Nacional de Historia, INAH, Mexico City. Photo: MZ.

casing a masterfully painted or sculpted image, *relicarios* generally were the product of a silversmith's workshop. The sacred memento within—a painting, print, relic, or minuscule image carved in ivory, wood, bone, or alabaster—might be supplied or created by the metal-smith himself, but particularly in the case of a finely crafted *relicario* painting or bas-relief, the memento was often the work of another master craftsman.

18th-century Mexican *relicario*, oil on copper paintings. Obverse: *San Ignacio Loyola*; reverse: *San Nicolás*, in gilded silver frame, 9.6 × 7.1 × 1.9 cm. Ex-Jake Gold collection, Santa Fe, New Mexico. Courtesy: Smithsonian Institution, Washington, D.C., catalogue # 176080. Photo: RS.

The frames of New Spain *relicarios* varied as widely as the contents of the lockets. The most common casement was a simple round or oval locket in brass, silver, or gold with a ring at the top for suspension. Sometimes a simple rope of twisted wire around the frame added decoration. New Spain *relicarios* were usually two-sided, with an image on each side protected behind discs of crystal, glass, or mica that were held in place by either a smooth- or tooth-edged bezel. The lockets were often relatively thick, perhaps 2 cm in width, providing for the storage of such personal mementos as a lock of hair or the scrap of a letter layered between the sacred images. Sometimes sheets of thick unadorned paper or fragments of playing cards are found inside these *relicarios*, materials that served as packing to keep the glass and images immobile within the locket.

Because of the popularity of devotional jewelry among the very wealthy during the colonial period, silver- and goldsmiths were often commissioned to craft exquisite one-of-a-kind *relicario* pendants in precious metals set with pearls and gems. Such lockets might be further embellished with enameling, chasing, repoussé, or filigree work. These pendants, sometimes rare masterpieces of colonial workmanship, were suspended from finely worked chains or hung from elegant *rosarios* of gold filigree beads, coral, jet, crystal, and other precious materials.

18th-century Mexican *relicario*. Two-sided carved and polychromed ivory medallion, 8 × 6 cm, in silver filigree pendant frame. Above: *San José con el Niño*; below: *San Jerónimo* and *San Francisco de Assisi*. Private collection. Photo: MZ.

The styles of *relicario* frames basically follow period styles of jewelry and the decorative arts of a country or region. Throughout the colonial period, for example, when gold and silver filigree work continued to be popular, the framing of *relicario* images was often in filigree. In the second half of the eighteenth century, when watches were much in vogue in New Spain, *relicario* lockets often resembled the casements of watches. Some were simple and of a base metal while others were elaborately worked in chased gold set with jewels. This fashion continued into the mid-nineteenth century in Mexico.

The most common kind of *relicario* in New Spain, as throughout the Americas, is a simply framed, two-sided pendant containing printed or painted religious images. These would have been inexpensive woodcuts or engravings, either imported from Europe or printed in the Americas. In New Spain, printing was introduced soon after the Conquest, with the earliest known book having been printed in Mexico City in 1539 (Weckman 1984, 617). Religious prints were a principal product of the presses of New Spain and were widely dis-

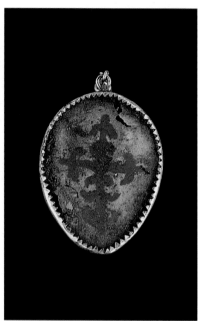

18th–19th-century Puerto Rican *relicario* containing pen-and-ink drawing of unidentified saint, and on the reverse, a cross. The *relicario* also contains bone and metal fragments, ashes, and clay. The silver frame is 5 cm in length. Teodoro Vidal Collection, San Juan, Puerto Rico. Photo: AR.

seminated. Because sometimes the prints contained in *relicarios* have been hand-colored, only close inspection tells whether the image is a print or hand drawn and painted. By the mid-nineteenth century, the use of prints as *relicario* images had been supplanted by chromolithographs and albumen photographs of favorite images.

Some *relicario* images of the saints, the Virgin, or Christ were exquisitely painted miniatures in oils on paper, vellum, or thin sheets of copper or silver. Watercolors painted on delicate slivers of cow bone or ivory were also popular, as were works on *nacar*—mother-of-pearl—and glass. In the nineteenth century in particular, religious images were sometimes painted in reverse on glass.

At least some of the Europeans who painted *relicarios* in the early days of the colonial period had been trained as illuminists in Europe. This is certainly true in the case of Luis Lagarto, one of the most famous New Spain painters of the *escudos de monja* (hagiographic badges worn by nuns), a type of *relicario* thought to be specific to the Americas. For seven decades beginning in the late sixteenth century, various members of the Lagarto family worked in Mexico City and later in Puebla, achieving renown as illuminists and painters of reliquary images.

In Spain, academic painters who executed large works on canvas for the church and Crown also sometimes painted miniatures for *relicarios*. Such renowned masters as Velázquez, Murillo, Goya, El Greco, and Bayeu painted miniatures, including those of religious themes (Ciancas and Meyer 1988, 13). In New Spain, such colonial painters as Cabrera, Ibarra, Serna, and José de Paez signed *escudos de monja*. They may have painted smaller *relicarios* as well. The art of the miniature was highly cultivated in New Spain (Sola 1935, 97).

Juan Correa (ca. 1645–1716), a Mexican mulatto who was one of the most prolific and respected artists of the Mexican baroque period, is also known to have painted *relicarios*. According to Fray Isidro Félix de Espinosa, writing his *Crónica de los Colegios de Propaganda Fide de la Nueva España* in 1746, in the last years of the seventeenth century, a fellow Franciscan, Francisco de Frutos, commissioned Juan Correa,

Mid-19th-century Mexican *relicario* in silver frame, 6.4 × 5.2 cm. Obverse: watercolor on vellum of *Santo Domingo Guzmán*; reverse: *Nuestra Señora de la Balvanera*, oil on copper. Within is a third image, an etching on vellum of Saint Ignacio. Courtesy Smithsonian Institution, Washington, D.C., catalogue # 298968.3. Photo: RS.

18th-century Mexican *relicario*. Oil on ivory in silver frame, 10×7 cm. Obverse: *La Virgen Inmaculada*; reverse: *San José con el Niño*. The Donald and Dorothy Cordry Collection at the Universidad Nacional Autónoma de México Museum, Mexico City. Photo: MZ.

18th-century Mexican *relicario*, oil on copper in gilded silver frame, 8.5 × 5.2 cm. Obverse: *El Divino Rostro*; reverse: *La Virgen de los Dolores*. Museo Nacional de Historia, INAH, Mexico City. Photo: MZ.

considered the *pintor guadalupano* (Guadalupe painter) of the period, to paint a large canvas of the Virgin for the Colegio de la Santa Cruz in Querétaro. At the same time, Fray Frutos asked Correa also to paint a small portable *relicario* of La Guadalupe for himself. In the time-honored manner of clerics, Father Frutos was probably able to obtain the *relicario de pilón*—as an extra—from Correa. Father Espinosa describes Fray Frutos's *relicario*: "To carry with him always, he obtained from the same painter another image, small, approximately one-sixth the size, painted on a shell and encased in a small box with glass, and on the two small doors, were painted kneeling images of the most glorious Patriarch Señor San José and N. P. [Our Patron] San Francisco. This image he carried hanging from his neck on all his journeys and in front of her he made all recite the holy rosary and chant the litany. He returned to the Colegio most pleased with his images (De Espinosa 1964, 511)."

The *relicario*, still in the hands of Mexican Franciscan fathers, consists of a simple but charming painting of the Guadalupe on an oyster shell 12.5 cm in diameter. It is encased in a wooden *nicho* that shows signs of having been worn about the neck from leather thongs. With the doors to this *nicho* open, the *relicario* container measures 28.5 cm by 16.5 cm by 6.5 cm.

Correa is thought to have painted the *nicho* as well as the *relicario* guarded within, although neither is signed. The inside of each of the

Juan Correa *relicario* of the Virgin of Guadalupe in its *nicho*, c. 1746. On the inside of the door to the left is *San José*; on the right, *San Francisco*.

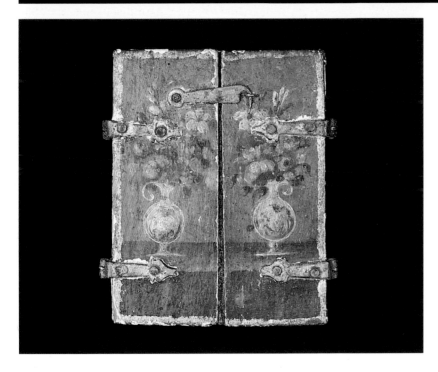

Juan Correa *nicho*, with its doors closed, c. 1746. Wear along the sides and back of the *nicho* indicate that the box itself was worn, probably suspended by cord or leather thong. Photo: AR.

18th-century Mexican *relicario*, oil on metal, of the Virgin of Guadalupe in silver frame, 7 × 5.8 cm. Private collection. Photo: A-S.

doors bears the image of a kneeling saint—San José and San Francisco, both well painted in the artist's typical style. The green exterior of the box is decorated with two urns of red roses.

Remarkably, the *relicario* and its *nicho* survived the many political and antichurch upheavals of post-Independence Mexico. Sometime around 1859, when the *Leyes de Reforma* (Reform Laws) mandated the closing of all of Mexico's monasteries and the wholesale confiscation of church property, the Franciscans of the Colegio de la Santa Cruz in Querétaro gave their monastery's valuables—paintings, images, sacred vessels, and this treasured Guadalupan *relicario*—to local families for safekeeping. Many of the items were never returned to the Franciscans, but about 1934 a descendant of one of the families that had been entrusted with the Colegio's valuables returned the Guadalupe *relicario* and its *nicho* to the Franciscans.

Father Frutos appears to have owned other *relicarios* as well. His engaging manner of procuring images of his patron, Nuestra Señora de Guadalupe, is described by Espinosa, who relates how Father Frutos came by another image of the Guadalupe that adorned his chambers: "This one he negotiated by means of entreaties and pleas (as it was much cherished by its owner), and to compel her, he extended to her an offer of spiritual bribery, that he would say some masses for her." Fray de Espinosa also mentions another *relicario* of La Guadalupe belonging to Fray Frutos: "Another [image] much smaller, about the size of a finger, made of *chalchiguite* (which is a stone that is easily worked), he kept in a small *relicario* (De Espinosa 1964, 512)."

While most religious pictures in colonial-period *relicarios* were either prints or paintings executed in oils or watercolors, some were featherwork mosaics. This pre-Hispanic art, called *amantecayotl*, was among the unique art forms practiced in the Americas at the time of the Conquest. The technique, originally used by the Aztecs for the decoration of shields, warriors' and priests' robes, and for making pictures, was primarily practiced in the regions of present-day Michoacán and Mexico City. *Amantecayotl* work, highly prized by the Aztecs, dazzled the Europeans upon their arrival.

In New Spain, the Spanish lords adapted featherwork techniques for the crafting of religious imagery, including that for *relicarios*. Feathers of the hummingbird, quetzal, various kinds of parrots, the heron, spoonbill, blue cotinga, and other birds created a striking and sometimes iridescent palette of colors for feather mosaics. At such schools

of mechanical arts as San José de los Naturales in Mexico City, founded by the Flemish Franciscan Pedro de Gante shortly after the Conquest, native artisans were trained in featherwork and produced religious works of remarkable quality.

This hispanicized Aztec craft reached its zenith in the sixteenth century, but by the seventeenth century the quality of featherwork paintings had declined to the point where the faces and hands of subjects often were painted rather than worked in feathers. By the beginning of the nineteenth century only a few *amantecas* (featherwork artisans) still practiced their art, in a much degenerated style (*Historia de Arte Mexicano, Vol. VI* 1982, 158).

Two exquisite seventeenth-century featherwork *relicarios*—one depicting the Virgen de los Remedios and the other a Pietà—are pre-

Two 17th-century Mexican featherwork mosaic *relicarios* in silver frames. The larger is approximately 8 cm in diameter. The *relicario* on the left depicts the *Virgen de los Relicarios*; on the right is a *Pietà*. Museo Nacional de Historia, INAH, Mexico City. Photo: MZ.

16th-century Mexican and European enameled-gold lantern pendant with pearls, 4 × 2.6 cm. The case is likely to have been made by a European, while the tiny boxwood sculptures protected by rock crystal are thought to be the work of Mexican Indians under the tutelage of Flemish and Spanish Jeronymite Fathers. The background is iridescent blue feathers. Six scenes are depicted: the Man of Sorrows (above) and St. Veronica (below); the Flagellation (above) and Christ Carrying the Cross (below); the Crucifixion and the Deposition. Walters Art Gallery, Baltimore.

served in Mexico City's Museo Nacional de Historia collection of miniatures.

The *relicarios* of New Spain sometimes contained fine religious miniature carvings in two-sided openwork ivory medallions, intricate boxwood tableaux, or simple bas-relief medallions in wood, plaster, or native alabaster, known as *tecali* in Mexico. Some of the most exquisite of these *relicario* carvings are boxwood reliefs dating from the sixteenth century. It is thought that these fine miniatures were the work of Mexican artisans trained by Spanish Jeronymite fathers. Sometimes these monochromatic boxwood miniatures were set against a background of finely worked iridescent blue or green feathers, to great effect. The few examples of this work that have survived attest to the exceptional quality and craftsmanship of these New Spain jewels.

The Walters Art Gallery in Baltimore has one such *relicario*, dating from the sixteenth century. It is a tiny lantern-style pendant of enameled gold and rock crystal framed by baluster columns crowned with seed pearls; another pearl dangles below the pendant, which measures 4 cm in length by 2.6 cm. On each side of the cube scenes in intricately carved boxwood are set against a backdrop of brilliant

17th-century silver and rock-crystal lantern pendant, Mexico, 4.5 × 2 cm, with carved boxwood relief sculptures on a ground of blue feathers on each of the four sides: the Virgin of the Rosary; the Crucifixion; and (not shown) the Resurrection; and the Descent from the Cross. Museo Nacional de Historia, INAH, Mexico City. Photo: MZ.

blue feathers. On one side is a tableau of the Crucifixion; on the reverse is a depiction of the Deposition. The lateral spaces between the two hold smaller two-tiered panels of Saint Veronica and the Flagellation and, opposite, the Man of Sorrows and Christ Carrying the Cross. The gold case itself may be of Spanish origins or it was crafted by a Spanish jeweler.

In the Museum of National History at Chapultepec Castle in Mexico City there is a similar lantern-style pendant, measuring 4.5 cm by 2 cm. The casing is simply constructed of silver and rock crystal and likewise contains four scenes carved in boxwood set against a background of iridescent blue feathers: the Crucifixion, the Deposition, the Resurrection, and an image of the Virgin of the Rosary.

The collections of the Louvre, the Metropolitan Museum of Art, and the Victoria and Albert Museum in London also include fine examples of these sixteenth- and seventeenth-century boxwood *relicarios* (Romero de Terreros 1990, 194).

By the beginning of the eighteenth century, *relicarios* with glazed- or rock-crystal panels encasing minutely carved boxwood and ivory

17th–18th-century Mexican *relicario* medallions carved in white wood that has been polychromed and gilded. The largest is 7.5 × 5.6 cm. Subjects depicted are *San Cristóbal, San Juan Bautista, Santa Bárbara*, and *San Mateo Evangelista*. Museo Franz Mayer, Mexico City. Photo: MZ.

figures, once a popular form throughout much of medieval Europe, were characteristic only of Spain and her colonies (*Gold and Silver of the Atocha and Santa Margarita* 1988, 189). Sometimes the boxwood relief was polychromed to simulate ivory (Muller 1972, 74).

Other hardwoods, especially orangewood, were used for the carving of *relicario* images in New Spain and elsewhere in the Americas. There are four such seventeenth- to eighteenth-century bas-relief medallions in the Franz Mayer Museum collection in Mexico City. The carvings, measuring between 6 cm and 7.5 cm in diameter, were sculpted of a light-colored wood and have been delicately polychromed and gilded. The depictions are of the Divino Pastor, San Mateo Evangelista, San Cristóbal, and Santa Bárbara.

Another popular medium for *relicario* carvings in New Spain was ivory. For two and a half centuries, ivory, both worked and raw, was one of the principal exports from the Philippines to New Spain and South America. From 1568 until 1815, when the Royal Philippine Company was abolished (Villegas 1983, 147), this galleon trade supplied the Americas with all manner of luxury goods, including devotional items made of ivory: crosses, rosaries, images of saints, covers for devotional books and missals, and other religious goods. Although the ship manifests of the Spanish galleons trading between the Orient and Acapulco were characteristically detailed, as required by the Crown, much of the worked ivory went unlisted. This may be because these were largely devotional items, overlooked by clerks by design or default (Sánchez Navarro de Pintado 1985, 58).

Although some of the surviving ivory *relicarios* of the Mexican colonial period appear to be of Indo-Portuguese or Ibero-Oriental style, in Mexico the carving of *relicarios* in ivory became a highly evolved art form during the viceregal period. While the carving of ivory in Mexico

could not compete in quality with the Chinese, Filipino, or Indo-Portuguese sculptures coming from Manila, the bas-relief *relicario* images were an exception. These were most typically round, elliptical, or octagonal double-sided medallions, between 4 and 6 cm in diameter (Sánchez Navarro de Pintado 1985, 120). These exquisite miniatures of the Virgin and the saints were finely carved in simple bas-relief or elaborate fretwork style (*calado*); additional detail was added with polychromed decoration and gilding. The medallions were then encased behind glass in lockets of silver or gold or in simple capsules of iron or tin.

There is no evidence of ivory workshops or guilds of ivory carvers in New Spain nor were there *ordenanzas* issued to govern such work. While there may have been Chinese and Filipino ivory carvers working in New Spain, *relicario* medallions were carved in New Spain by local craftsmen, most likely in Mexico City and in Puebla. "Of this

Mexican *relicario*, 1749. Frame of repoussé, chased and enameled gold, with polychromed and gilded medallion of carved bone. Approximately 12 cm in diameter. Obverse: *Santa Gertrudis*; reverse: unknown bishop at his death. Museo Nacional de Historia, INAH, Mexico City. Photo: MZ.

18th-century Mexican *relicario* bas-relief medallion, carved and polychromed ivory, 5 × 4.2 cm. Obverse: *La Purísima Concepción*; reverse: *San José con el Niño*. Museo Nacional de Historia, INAH, Mexico City. Photo: MZ.

18th-century Mexican *relicario*, octagonal bas-relief medallion of polychromed and gilded ivory in circular frame of silver, 7.7 × 6 cm. Obverse: *San José con el Niño*; reverse: *La Virgen con el Niño*. Museo Nacional de Historia, INAH, Mexico City. Photo: MZ.

type there definitely are examples of unmistakable Mexican workmanship," Romero de Terreros says (1951, 122).

In pre-Columbian times, native craftsmen had carved exquisite tiny objects in teeth and bone of the jaguar, deer, boar, and mountain goat (Keleman 1969, 250), and the sixteenth-century boxwood carvers clearly show the abilities of New Spain artisans to create fine works. Although most pieces were unsigned, some New Spain ivory carvers have been identified. In the early seventeenth century, an Indian named Juan de la Cruz worked ivory in Puebla. Between 1649 and 1660 an artisan named Marcos Espinosa worked ivory and ebony (Sánchez Navarro de Pintado 1985, 119). Pál Keleman, the renowned art historian of the Americas, mentions a carved ivory *relicario* signed by a Mercedarian monk. The small plaque, with a richly carved Virgen del Rosario, complete with all her attributes, carried an inscription on the reverse: "Diego de Reinoso y Sandoval made me in the City of Mexico 1637 (Keleman 1969, 250)." Francisco de la Maza describes a carved and polychromed alabaster oval 25 cm in diameter of the Purisima, similarily inscribed: *Diego Reinoso y Sandoval me fecit en la siudad de Mexico, 1651* (De la Maza 1966, 84). Although he did not sign his work, it is known that José Fuentes de María, a Spaniard traveling with an American passport who arrived in Mexico in 1830, worked in Puebla until his death in 1874 as a miniaturist specializing in the carving of religious miniatures in ivory (Ciancas and Meyer 1988, 25).

In New Spain, some unique materials were employed in the fashioning of *relicarios*. Tiny images and bas-relief medallions were sculpted in *tecali*, an alabaster native to the district of the same name in the state of Puebla. Similar work was done in highland Peru in the local alabaster, *piedra huamanga*. As with ivory and wood carvings, the alabaster reliefs of New Spain were sometimes polychromed and gilded. De la Maza says that there must have been quantities of small alabaster sculptures, given the number of them that have survived (De la Maza 1966, 89).

The Museo Nacional de Historia in Mexico City has one of the largest known collections of New Spain *relicarios*. In New Spain the most common subjects for *relicario* painters are images of the Virgin Mary—La Guadalupe, La Dolorosa, La Balvanera, La Encarnación, La Inmaculada Concepción, El Inmaculado Corazón de María, La Merced, La Virgen del Refugio, and others. Christ is also a popular subject: El Sagrado Corazón, Con la Cruz a Cuestas, Cristo de la Columna, Cristo Crucificado, Ecce Homo, El Niño Jesús, and the Divino Rostro. Saints commonly depicted are San Francisco de Assisi, San Francisco Javier, San Francisco de Paula, Santa Gertrudis, San Ignacio, San José con el Niño, San Pedro Apóstol, and Santa Rosalía.

The overall popularity of religious jewelry declined following Mexico's independence from Spain in 1821. The church, whose power and destiny had been intertwined with that of the Crown during the colonial era, found itself stripped of its influence and possessions in independent Mexico, and the country was swept by recurrent waves of anticlericism into the 1930s. The practice of religion retreated into the privacy of church interiors and homes.

In independent Mexico, women's jewelry reflected the mood of the age, which was antichurch and increasingly secularized. Romanticism replaced piety as the popular sentiment. Mexican women of fashion were more likely to wear portrait miniatures of loved ones or classical heroes rather than images of the saints while devout women and some men continued to wear religious jewelry, albeit less publicly. Some exceptionally fine *relicarios* were made during the nineteenth century, often by painters who worked in the popular portrait miniature genre. One of the finest of these miniaturists was Francisco Morales Van den Eynden Morales (1811–1884), a prolific painter who worked in Puebla, where he produced some two hundred miniatures, many of religious images and themes (Ciancas and Meyer 1988, 25).

Independent Mexico and Central America saw many social changes that affected the practice of religion and the use of *relicarios*.

17th-century Mexican *relicario*, medallion of carved hard white stone, probably native alabaster, in silver frame 4.3 cm in length. Obverse: *San Antonio*; reverse (not shown): *San Juan Bautista*. Museo Franz Mayer, Mexico City. Photo: MZ.

18th-century Mexican *relicario*. Bas-relief medallion is of carved alabaster or plaster, polychromed and gilded, in gilded metal frame, 8.7 × 6.7 cm. Obverse: *La Virgen de la Soledad*; reverse: *San Francisco Assisi*. Museo Nacional de Historia, INAH, Mexico City. Photo: MZ.

18th–19th-century Mexican *relicario*, carved, sculpted, and polychromed wax in gold frame, 6.5 × 4.5 cm. Obverse: *La Virgen María*; reverse: *San Juan Bautista*. Museo Nacional de Historia, INAH, Mexico City. Photo: MZ.

Indians, once forbidden to wear Spanish fashions, took to wearing them toward the end of colonial rule when such restrictions were not enforced. In the post-Independence period the Indian women of Mexico and Central America, particularly those living in isolated regions, wore Spanish devotional jewelry after such fashion was passé among the Creole and mestiza women of Mexico. The popularity of religious jewelry among native women continued into the second half of the twentieth century when urbanization, "westernization," and the evangelical Protestant movement rendered the wearing of such devotional jewelry unfashionable.

American folklorists Donald and Dorothy Cordry collected a number of *relicarios* in their travels throughout rural Indian Mexico in the first half of the twentieth century. "Most of the villages in the eighteenth century used *relicarios* with cases of silver or silver gilt, containing pictures of saints usually painted on tin, bone or ivory," the Cordrys relate. "As *relicarios* are usually about ½ inch in thickness, one finds pieces of old documents or religious printed matter used as filling. If a date is found on the old paper, it is usually from the middle of the eighteenth century. The case of one *relicario* in our collection is decorated with enamel. The Choapan girl [pictured] wears a similar one, without enamel (Cordry and Cordry 1978, 158)."

In Mexico it was customary to place personal mementos in *relicarios*, sandwiched between religious prints or paintings. According to José Amador Pérez, a Mexican silversmith who still makes *relicarios* and other religious jewelry in his Cholula workshop, typical memorabilia found in *relicarios* include family photographs; grains of sand from La Villa (the shrine to Our Lady of Guadalupe outside Mexico City); fragments of clothing from a loved one; a piece of palm frond from Palm Sunday; a *chinito*—a lock of a child's hair, especially from his first haircut; a handwritten note; and so on. Because Mexican *relicarios* are often used as casements for personal mementos as well as for religious imagery, they are sometimes referred to as *guardapelos*, lockets for the treasuring of a lock of hair (and other items); (Interview, Belen, N.M., March 1991).

In postcolonial Mexico and Central America, *relicarios*, as well as other religious mementos, were available from a variety of sources. Specially crafted *relicarios* were usually commissioned from a local silversmith. In such traditional jewelry-producing centers as Puebla, Tuxtla Gutiérrez, Toluca, Oaxaca, Pátzcuaro, Iguala, San Cristóbal de

Zapotec Indian woman from Santiago Choapan, Oaxaca, Mexico, wearing three 18th-century *relicarios* and other traditional religious jewelry. The photograph was taken by Donald Cordry in 1941. Courtesy Arizona State Museum, Tucson.

las Casas, Taxco, and Mexico City, jewelers continue to make all manner of religious goods for their traditional customers. Additionally, religious-goods vendors, whose stalls are set up in front of churches and pilgrimage sites or in the *tianguis* on market day, provide the faithful with inexpensive devotional items, including framed holy pictures for wearing that could be considered a degenerated version of colonial-period *relicarios*.

Itinerant peddlers were once a source for devotional items such

19th–20th-century New Mexican tin and mica *relicarios*. The largest is 4.6×3.1 cm. Ward Minge Collection, Corrales, New Mexico. Photo: AR.

as *relicarios*, even as far north as New Mexico. In 1941, as part of the Works Progress Administration's Writers' Project, Lou Sage Batchen interviewed elderly residents of Placitas, New Mexico, who told of itinerant Arab peddlers periodically passing through their village during the mid-nineteenth century on their way to the gold mine at San Pablo (Golden). These olive-skinned, barefooted peddlers came to the village in twos or threes, wearing long flowing robes and turbans. They exchanged religious trinkets for the villagers' chile, wheat, goats, and hides: "These were the things for which the villagers would part with their last tortilla and the peddlers knew it (Batchen 1941)." By the 1870s the *árabes* were still visiting the isolated mountain villages of New Mexico, but they wore the dress of the day, and they now expected cash for their goods (Batchen 1941).

A popular form of *relicario* in New Mexico in the late nineteenth and early twentieth centuries was the small, rectangular, tin-framed religious print, preserved behind a sheet of mica and with a loop at the back for hanging. An artisan in Peña Blanca, a village along the Rio Grande midway between Albuquerque and Santa Fe, made many such devotional items. Some were shaped like tiny books, with a punched tin cover and a print within. Similar homemade framed images, with a loop at the top for suspension, can also be found in many parts of Latin America.

18th-century Mexican *escudo de monja* (nun's escutcheon). Oil on canvas of the Virgin of Guadalupe with the Trinity and numerous saints, framed in tortoise shell, 9.2 cm in diameter. Private collection. Photo: A-S.

4 _ESCUDOS DE MONJA_: A GENRE OF NEW SPAIN _RELICARIOS_

OR THE UPPER-CLASS WOMen of New Spain there were but two honorable life paths open to them: marriage and the convent. While many of these women happily accepted marriages that were arranged for them most typically by the men in their families, many girls and women chose convent life instead. They did so, in many cases, out of piety and a sense of true religious vocation, but convent life also provided an escape from the prospect of undesirable marriages.

The daily life of a nun was not that dissimilar from that of married women and girls living in their own homes. Given the piety and conservatism of the age, much of women's lives was already linked to religious activities, and they enjoyed little personal freedom. Especially in the sixteenth and seventeenth centuries, convent women often lived well. They had their own quarters, complete with servants, pupils, and female companions. They enjoyed a fair amount of freedom to pursue their own interests in music, drama, painting, sculpture, literature, theology, and scholarship. The women religious of the colonial period were also renowned for their excellence in such traditional female occupations as embroidery, needlework, the culinary arts, gardening, medicine, and herbology.

Nuns also owned and managed valuable properties and businesses. They were most commonly engaged in selling goods produced behind the cloistered walls. Invariably, nuns made a variety of devotional items for sale to the public as well as for their own use. Throughout the Americas, religious women made *relicarios*, or at least the imagery within the lockets, and wore them as part of their habits.

Early-seventeenth-century New Spain Conceptionist and Jeronymite nuns wore a unique type of *relicario* that came to be called the *escudo de monja*, or nun's escutcheon. These hagiographic badges were also called *medallones* (medallions) or simply *placas* (plaques). The *escudos* were generally circular or oval discs of vellum or sheets of copper, 15 to 20 cm in diameter, that were framed in silver, mother-of-pearl (*nacar*), tortoiseshell (*carey*), or wood. On them a nun's particular devotions to the Virgin and the saints were painted in oils or watercolor. In some cases, these saints represented the name saints of a woman's family; their presence on the *escudo* was intended to remind the nun to pray for the spiritual well-being of her relatives. In general, the central figure in an *escudo* would be an avocation of the Virgin—the Annunciation, Our Lady of the Rosary, the Immaculate Conception, the Virgin of the Apocalypse, Our Lady of Guadalupe—surrounded by angels and saints to whom the nun was particularly devoted. Less common than the oil on copper *escudos* were those done in watercolors on vellum, protected in their frames by glass. *Escudos* were worn as brooches, fastened to the nun's habit just beneath her chin by clips, rings, or cord (Muriel de la Torre and Romero de Terreros 1952, 203).

While the exact origins of the *escudo de monja* are unknown, the badges are thought to have been unique to the New World (Tovar de Teresa 1988, 176). It could be argued that the *escudos* bear some relationship to the popular late-medieval Spanish custom of *veneras*, badges denoting religious affiliation worn by members of religious orders and lay societies (*cofradías*). While the *veneras* were most often symbolical insignia, sometimes they were pictographic as well. As Muller describes these seventeenth-century *veneras*, "During fiestas honoring La Inmaculada members of the Confraternities of the Conception . . . wore on silken ribbons at their necks enameled gold images of the Virgin (Muller 1972, 121)."

The Conceptionist order was not only the first to be established in New Spain, it also became the most widely diffused religious order for women throughout the Americas (Lopétegui and Zubillaga 1965, 872). The first novitiates in the Convento de la Concepción in Mexico City included daughters of the *conquistadores* (Muriel de la Torre 1946,

Mid-18th-century Mexican *escudo de monja*. Oil on copper in tortoiseshell frame, 17.4 cm in diameter. Spanish Colonial Arts Society Collections on loan to the Museum of New Mexico at the Museum of International Folk Art, Santa Fe, New Mexico. Photo: AR.

18th-century Mexican *escudo de monja, La Inmaculada Concepción*. Silk-thread embroidery with faces painted in oils in tortoiseshell frame, 13 cm in diameter. Museo Franz Mayer, Mexico City. Photo: MZ.

33), and only wealthy white women born in Spain or in the Americas of Spanish parents were admitted (Muriel de la Torre 1946, 29). Although the Conceptionists took vows of poverty, obedience, and chastity, life in their cloisters was not without its comforts. In the early period, the Conceptionist nuns lived in large individual "cells" together with servants who cooked and cleaned for them, girls entrusted to their care, and *favorecidas* (Muriel de la Torre 1946, 38). The ostentation of wealth which came to characterize the Spanish colonists' style of life did not stop at the convent gates. According to Marroquí, "the fondness for luxuries had also penetrated the cloister walls (Carrillo y Gariel 1959, 185)." The Conceptionist habit was elegant. "They wore a tunic and scapulary of white serge, a mantle of a clear blue color. On the breast, on top of the scapulary, and on top of the mantle on the right side they wore two *escudos* with religious images. At the waist they tied a hemp cord, and completing the vestment were a white coif and wimple and the black veil (Carrillo y Gariel 1959, 188)."

17th-century Mexican *escudo de monja*. Silk embroidery of the Coronation of the Virgin with faces painted in oils. Gold-leaf wood frame, 23 × 28 cm. Museo Franz Mayer, Mexico City. Photo: MZ.

17th-century Mexican *escudo de monja*, 18 cm in diameter, embroidered with silver and silk thread on silk background. "The Coronation of the Virgin." Museo Franz Mayer, Mexico City. Photo: MZ.

Conceptionist nuns also wore an additional badge on the right shoulder. This *escudo*, virtually identical in size and style to that worn on the chest, was embroidered rather than painted. The working of these badges was exquisite and thought to have been done by the nuns themselves. Embroidery was a principal activity in most convents, and one on which the nuns lavished much time, skill, and devotion. When it was not possible for a nun to finely detail in silk thread the faces and hands of religious personages, she would paint these components on paper or vellum and incorporate them into the embroidery of her *escudo*. The background of these embroidered badges was often a *petatillo* (crosshatch design) in gold or silver thread (Muriel de la Torre and Romero de Terreros 1952, 204).

Embroidered *escudos* were also known to have been made by men in the eighteenth century. Fray Juan Galindo and Fray Andrés Nazari of the monastery of Nuestra Señora de la Merced in Mexico City were renowned for their mastery in embroidering *escudos* (Romero de Terreros 1923, 187). In Spain itself, embroidery was a highly developed

18th-century Mexican *escudos de monja*. Oil on copper paintings in tortoiseshell frames. The oval *escudo*, 21 × 17 cm, depicting the Annunciation is signed *José de Paez fecit* (c. 1720–1790). The round *escudo*, 18 cm in diameter, of the Crowning of the Virgin by the Trinity is signed Manuel Serna, active in Mexico City about 1690–1700. Hispanic Society of America, New York.

art among monks, and the region of Granada in particular was known for its Renaissance embroideries: priests' vestments, altar cloths, banners and *veneras* for the religious societies, and so on.

It is unclear which type of *escudos de monja*—the painted or the embroidered variety—was first used. Romero de Terreros speculates that embroideries preceded the paintings on copper, but the latter variety of *escudos* came to be more common due to the high cost of the silk embroidery floss and the time involved in embroidering an *escudo* (Romero de Terreros 1923, 188).

The use of the *escudo de monja* may have later been adopted in New Spain by nuns other than the Conceptionists and Jeronymites or by members of *cofradías* as well. An anonymous portrait of the Augustinian nun Madre María Agustina Rodríguez de Pedroso, who took the habit in the Convent of San Bernardo in Mexico on 23 May 1799, depicts her wearing a circular *escudo* identical to those associated with the Conceptionist and Jeronymite orders (Muriel de la Torre and Romero de Terreros 1952, 34).

While the *escudos de monja* were most commonly associated with the nuns of New Spain, it is possible that they were also worn by nuns in Peru. Sor Inés Muñóz de Rivera, foundress of the Convento de la Concepción in Lima and sister-in-law of Francisco Pizarro from her first marriage, is shown in an anonymous portrait dated 1632 wearing a New Spain–style painted *escudo* beneath her chin (Muriel de la Torre and Romero de Terreros 1952, 203).

In the chronicle of his travels through seventeenth-century Peru, the Franciscan Fray Isidro Félix de Espinosa describes the elegant habits of the Peruvian Conceptionists: "[They wear] white habits, and blue mantles with the insignia, and an image of Our Lady on the breast and another on the mantle at the shoulder (De Espinosa 1964, 409)." Unfortunately, De Espinosa does not describe the Peruvian *escudos* in sufficient detail for us to be able to determine if they were analogous to those worn in Mexico. In all likelihood, the wearing of large Mexican-style *escudos* was not common in Peru. We do know that in the convents of the Viceroyalty of Peru, the use of smaller-scale *relicarios* was universal (De Mesa and Gisbert 1990, 13).

Portraits of New Spain nuns show them wearing their *escudos*. In the late eighteenth century, portraits of *monjas coronadas*, nuns "crowned" with huge floral headdresses, became a popular genre of painting that commemorated the beginning or terminus of a woman's consecrated life or served to mark an important event in the convent's

Early 19th-century unsigned oil on canvas portrait of Sor María Gertrudis de Corazón de Jesús, Conceptionist nun who took vows at the Royal Convent of Jesús María in Mexico City. The nun is wearing an *escudo* of the Annunciation. Museo Nacional del Virreinato, INAH, Tepozotlán, Mexico.

history. These lyrical portraits frequently portrayed the nuns wearing *escudos* at their throats; sometimes, in the case of Conceptionist nuns, the embroidered *escudo* on the right shoulder is also discernible.

In the eighteenth century such paintings were often commissioned by the women's proud pious families who might never see their cloistered daughters again, depending on the order's rules. Hung on the walls of the family home, these portraits served to commemorate the "mystical marriage" of a daughter to the Savior, as nuns traditionally consider themselves brides of Christ. In a stanza of her poem that describes a nun's profession of vows, "Sacred Letters for the Solemn Occasion of a Nun's Profession of Vows," Sor Juana Inés de la Cruz (1651–1695), New Spain's most illustrious woman of letters, describes "huge jewels" as part of a nun's costume on this occasion; it is thought that the poetess was referring to the *escudos*:

Dióme, en fe, su anillo,
Y de su desposorio,

Y de inmensas joyas
Compuso mi adorno.
(De la Cruz 1989, 319)

In faith and troth of his vow,
He bestowed on me his ring.
And with immense jewels
He completed my adornment.

The *monjas coronadas* portraits that were painted at the time of a nun's death were generally commissioned by the woman's order. These portraits were hung on convent walls to commemorate the exemplary lives, virtues, and accomplishments of the convent's important women.

Not all Conceptionist or Jeronymite women wore *escudos*, however. Recent excavations of the Convent of San Jerónimo in downtown Mexico City show that many, but not all, Jeronymite nuns were interred wearing *escudos*. It is likely that the nuns who wore these jewels to their graves were the more important figures in the convent, such as the abbesses, bursars, and mistresses of novices (Cuellar and Cordero 1992).

In New Spain, *escudos de monja* were painted by the nuns themselves as well as by amateur or professional artists. Some are works by the renowned artists of the day and have been considered masterpieces of viceregal-period artistic expression. Although many *escudos* were painted in anonymity, some were signed. Colonial-period painters such as José de Ibarra, Miguel Cabrera, Miguel de Herrera, Patricio Morlete Ruíz, José de Paez, Juan de Paez, Manuel Serna, José de Alcíbar, Carlos and Andres López, and Juan Antonio Vallejo are known to have painted *escudos*. In the collections of the Museo Nacional de Historia in Mexico City, numerous *escudos* are signed by painters about whom little is known: María Concepción Fernández, Navarrete, José Santos Pensado, Tafalla, and others.

Various portraits of Sor Juana, the most famous Jeronymite nun, invariably show her wearing an *escudo de monja*. It is possible that Sor Juana herself may have painted her own *escudo*, as in addition to being one of the greatest poets of the Hispanic world she was also an accomplished artist (Muriel de la Torre 1946, 493).

Some of the finest examples of nuns' *escudos* are those attributed to various members of the Lagarto family of Mexico City and Puebla. Luis Lagarto, a Spanish illuminist and teacher who was in New Spain by 1585, has been called the finest miniaturist of his time in the Hispanic world (Tovar de Teresa 1988, 15). Although Lagarto, his sons,

and grandsons were best known for their illumination of manuscripts and their decoration of the Cathedral in Puebla, they also created exquisite reliquary images such as Agnus Dei and *escudos*.

One example of the Lagarto *escudos*, a circular watercolor on vellum in a tortoiseshell frame that is now in the Robert H. Lamborn Collection at the Philadelphia Museum, is thought to have been painted either by Andrés Lagarto (1589–1666) or his brother Luis de la Vega Lagarto (1586–d. after 1631). In either case, the work appears to have been painted in the mid-seventeenth century.

It is not known how long the custom of the *escudos de monja* endured nor how far from Mexico City their use among women of religious orders extended. Various museums and private collections have examples of Mexican oil on copper *escudos* in a late baroque style that would seem to indicate that the custom endured at least into the early nineteenth century. In Mexico, as elsewhere in the Americas, the secular nature of the Wars for Independence and a growing anticlerical sentiment among colonists made the wearing of showy religious jewelry unfashionable by the late eighteenth century. Even behind cloister walls women religious were unlikely to have been impervious to popular sentiments or fashion.

Verdadero Retrato de la Hermosissima Imagen de Nro Señor Crucificado . . . ese ob d que se Venera en el Convento antiguo de Señoras Carmelitas de alla de la Ciudad de Mexico.

18th-century oil on canvas painting of the *Cristo de Santa Teresa* by José de Ibarra (1688–1756). The legend at the bottom of the painting reads, "Faithful portrait of the most beautiful image of Our Crucified Lord . . . that is venerated in old Convent of the Carmelite Sisters in the City of Mexico." This miraculous image of Christ appeared in Ixmiquilpan. In the background are four Agnus Dei medallions. Museo Nacional del Virreinato, INAH, Tepotzotlán, Mexico.

5 THE AGNUS DEI: A *RELICARIO* TRADITION IN WAX

MONG THE *RELICARIOS* OF Spain and New Spain there is a type of wearable reliquary that has its own specific characteristics and history: the *Agnus Dei*. These are reliquary lockets that contain wax seals stamped with the image of the Lamb of God, or *Agnus Dei*, a symbol for Christ, the "sacrificial lamb." They are most commonly encased in simple or elaborate frames and protected by glass that affords the viewing of both sides of the wax disc. From the Middle Ages into the nineteenth century, Agnus Dei lockets were worn by the devout women of Catholic Europe, whether common folk or royalty. Mary Queen of Scots, for example, is said to have worn a rock-crystal Agnus Dei to her beheading in 1587. These devotional pendants were particularly popular in Spain, Portugal, and their colonies.

The Agnuses were part of the popular culture and beliefs that the Iberian settlers transported to the Americas with them. Wills, inventories, and pawn tickets of the colonial period frequently list these religious medallions among the prized possessions and valuables of the colonists.

It appears that the custom of wearing Agnus Dei lockets dates to at least the fourteenth century in Europe. The inventories of the Queen of France in 1372 and of Charles VI in 1399 include Agnus Dei pendants. One such fourteenth-century piece, a wax roundel that

18th-century Mexican Agnus Dei wax medallion in silver frame, 9.5×7.5 cm. Obverse: an image of the Agnus Dei; reverse: an image identified as "Saint Basil Great Bishop of Cesarea (A.D. 329–379) Innocent XIII." Private collection. Photo: MZ.

was issued by Pope Urban VI between 1378 and 1389 encased in a fifteenth-century German case, is preserved in the Victoria and Albert Museum (Evans 1989, 50). In the seventeenth century, the French Countess d'Aulnoy, who visited Madrid during the reign of Charles II, mentions the Agnus in her description of the jewelry worn by Spanish women: "They also wear the agnus, together with little images about their neck and arms, or in their hair (Williams 1908, 109)."

Beginning perhaps as early as the fourth century, fragments of the unused portions of a previous year's Easter candles from the chapels, basilicas, and churches of Rome were sold as devotional souvenirs to the faithful on Holy Saturday (Quintana 1965, 13). In the sixth century, these wax mementos were given their characteristic round shape. The wax was mixed with holy oils and molded into medallions, possibly in imitation of the treasured Roman *bullae*—discs of gold or other materials worn about the neck by Roman youths. Some suggest that the promotion of the Agnus was an attempt by the church to counter the persistent pagan belief in the amuletic power of the *bullae* (Romero de Terreros 1990, 179). The wax roundel also bore a resemblance to the consecrated host preserved behind glass in a monstrance; sometimes such hosts were imprinted with the Agnus Dei image.

The name "Agnus Dei" ("Lamb of God") refers to the image of the paschal lamb grasping a cross in its forelegs—the Cross of the Redemption upon which the Lamb (Christ) was sacrificed. He is commonly posed on the book of the Seven Seals. The aureola behind the Lamb's head indicates his divinity. The reverse side of the wax disc bears the image of a saint, the Virgin in one of her advocations, or other religious themes.

In its truest form, the Agnus was issued by a pope during the first year of his reign and every seven years thereafter (Muller 1972, 50). One side or the other of the Agnus bore the name of the pope, his coat of arms, and the year of his pontification. The holy personages depicted on the medallion's reverse side were indicative of the pope's particular hagiographic devotions (Quintana 1965, 14).

Originally, the Agnus waxes were blessed by the archdeacon and on the Saturday before Easter Week were distributed to the faithful, especially those recently baptized. Later the blessing of the Agnus was done by the pope himself (Romero de Terreros 1990, 179).

In the years of the Counter-Reformation, the Agnus Dei medallions were very popular, and a great variety of them were made (Tovar

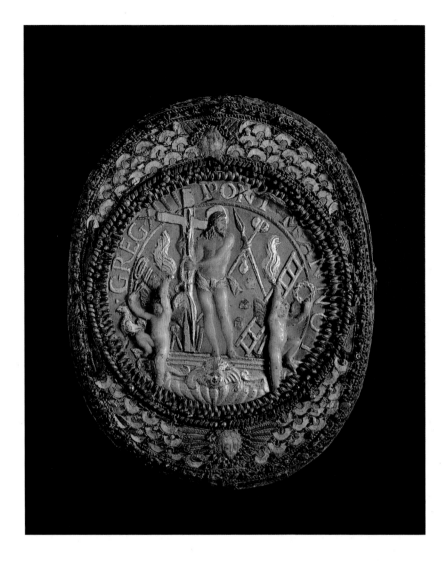

16th–17th-century Agnus Dei polychromed and gilded-wax medallion in embroidered frame, 21.9 × 17.2 cm, embellished with glass beads, metallic thread, and sequins. The image depicted is Christ with symbols of the Passion. The inscription in Latin reads "Gregory XIII in the first year of his papacy (1572)." Private collection. Photo: MZ.

de Teresa 1988, 189). The early Agnuses were made in the Vatican itself, but due to irregularities and difficulties, Pope Paul V in 1608 entrusted the task to the Cistercian monks of the Basilica of the Holy Cross of Jerusalem in Rome, who still make them (Quintana 1965, 15). A number of Agnus Dei are preserved in the basilica's treasury, including some decorated with relics of the Passion (Quintana 1965, 19).

Although the Agnuses were originally round in form, later ones were sometimes ovaloid. They varied in size from 1 cm to 20 cm in diameter. Beginning in the late Middle Ages when devotional jewelry was in high fashion, the Agnuses were often preserved in luxurious cartouches of cloth. Later they were encased in *relicarios* of gold, silver, calamine, or brass, with two crystals that allowed both sides of the Agnus to be visible. Thin sheets of transparent horn sometimes were used for the same purpose (Newman 1981, 13). The Agnuses were also framed in wood and decorated in a variety of artistic ways. Such work was typically done by nuns or monks (Quintana 1965, 19). In New Spain and later in the republican period of Mexican history, the Agnus waxes were encased in sumptuous lockets of precious metals and jewels, as well as in simple brass casings. Large Agnus Dei that were polychromed, gilded, decorated with beads and pearls, and preserved in elaborate frames were sometimes hung in the home or around the image of a favorite saint as a votive offering. The small, unadorned Agnus waxes, however, were most typically encased in medallions and worn by devout women as pendants or as part of *rosario* necklaces.

Throughout the Iberian world there were a number of folk beliefs surrounding the Agnus. In fourteenth-century Europe, Agnus Dei set in silver bezels were worn most typically by women during their pregnancies (Muller 1972, 50). In the Philippines, early Spanish missionaries used the Agnus extensively for faith-healing purposes. This served two purposes: it counteracted the medicinal activities of the powerful native *babylans* (shamans); and it readily attracted converts to Christianity (Villegas 1983, 120). In twentieth-century Colombia, small devotional pendants containing tiny wax flowers and a sacred image within were colloquially called "agnus," although they did not actually contain the Agnus wax medallions. These religious amulets were pinned on the insides of children's clothing to protect them from harm.

Quintana lists the properties traditionally attributed to the Agnus Dei by the faithful in Mexico: "They have diverse virtues: they provoke feelings of recognition of God's goodness, they increase grace, enhance piety, erase venial sins, free one from temptation, prevent sudden death, give protection against adversity, keep one safe in war, prevent diseases and serve as remedies, combat pestilence and airborne disease; they calm the winds, hurricanes and tempests, they save one from shipwreck; they prevent fires; they have virtues against torrential rains, flooding and rivers overflowing their banks (Quintana 1965, 17)."

The Agnus Dei were a popular item of devotional jewelry throughout Spain's colonies, as evidenced by their appearance in numerous inventories of personal possessions and their mention in the literature of the colonial period. Church inventories also often list them, usually as gifts (*presentallas*) to a saint or, most commonly, to the Virgin. In a Caracas inventory dated 1621 that lists jewelry belonging to the wife of Francisco de Castillo, three Agnus Dei are mentioned and described: "an a[g]nus dei in gold with emeralds weighing 2 ounces and six long *ochavos*. An anus [*sic*] decorated with enameled gold weighing one ounce and two and a half *ochavos*. Another a[g]nus in crystal with filigreed gold weighing 1 ounce (Duarte 1970, 55)." The inventory of Mexico City resident Clara Henríquez's jewelry, taken in 1602, lists an elegant Agnus: "An Agnus Dei in gold, large, frosted, made by nuns' hands, hanging from a rosary of thick corals tipped with gold (Toussaint 1948, 176)."

Even in such far-flung corners of the Spanish Empire as San Antonio, Texas, women colonists treasured these sacred mementos. The 1787 will of María Josefa Granados lists among her personal possessions "two gold *relicarios* each with their wax agnus; and another small one of the same style (Granados 1787)."

The Agnus Dei, along with other types of devotional items, were carried by the Spanish as trade goods into even the most remote areas of their colonies. In 1598 Juan de Oñate, traveling north into present-day New Mexico with several hundred troops, settlers, and clergy, carried a variety of glass beads, bead necklaces, rosaries, and "thirty-three Agnus Dei of tin and gold, appraised at 6 *tomines* each, 24 *pesos* and 2 *tomines* (Hammond and Rey 1953, 135)." In recounting his journey from San Juan de Ulloa (Veracruz) to Mexico City in 1625, the English Dominican priest Thomas Gage mentions giving Agnus Dei and other devotional items to Indians in thanks for their hospitality to his party (Gage 1648, 25).

The use of the Agnus was subjected to periodic regulations by ecclesiastical authorities. In 1572 Pope Gregory XIII (1572–1585), in an effort to maintain the symbolically pure white color of the Agnus, issued a papal bull prohibiting the gold-leafing, coloration, or painting of Agnus Dei medallions; violators were subject to excommunication

18th-century Agnus Dei wax medallion in silver frame, 8.5 × 6 cm. Images and legends are no longer readable. UNAM Museum, Mexico City. Gift of Donald and Dorothy Cordry.

(Quintana 1965, 17). (It was unusual for the Agnus to contain actual relics, but sometimes the paschal candle from which the Agnus was formed had been coated with a powder made from the dust of saints' bones, and the wax was consequently grayish in color.)

The existence of illuminated Agnus Dei from the period amply suggests that this law, like so many issued by the Crown and church authorities during the colonial period in New Spain, was largely ignored. The polychroming and gilding of Agnus Dei were common practices in New Spain, and the church was making an attempt, however futile, to combat such practices.

One such beautifully decorated Agnus, a large central Agnus Dei medallion surrounded by four smaller ones, has been attributed to the Lagarto family. The dates stamped on this Agnus, the year XIII of the reign of Pope Paul V (1605–1621), indicate that the medallions were issued in 1618 (Tovar de Teresa 1988, 189).

The ecclesiastical prohibitions against the painting of the Agnus extended to Spain as well. A Badajoz inventory of 1589 describes a gold-mounted "illuminated a.d.," an Agnus Dei painted in illuminist detail. The same inventory also lists an Agnus of crystal set in gold with gold "stamps" of the Virgin and San Francisco (Muller 1972, 73). The use of the term "Agnus Dei" was probably used popularly to refer not only to the paschal wax seals issued by the papacy but perhaps to other types of *relicarios* as well.

During the colonial period, the Agnus Dei existed in great quantity in New Spain and elsewhere in the Americas, yet few have survived the vicissitudes of time. Because they were of wax, a material that could easily melt or be consumed by insects, only a few Agnus Dei from the colonial period can be found in the treasuries of old churches and convents or in Spanish colonial art collections.

Second half of the 18th century Agnus Dei reliquary, 44 × 37.5 cm. Carved, gilded, and polychromed wood with mother-of-pearl incrustation. Medallions contain relics and Agnus Dei waxes. Private collection. Photo: MZ.

Late 17th–early 18th-century oil on canvas painting from Altoperu, "The Virgin and the Christ Child." Attributed to the School of Leonardo Flores. 244 × 142 × 71 cm. Mount Calvary Retreat House, The Order of the Holy Cross, Santa Barbara, California. Photo: TP.

6
THE *RELICARIOS* OF SPANISH SOUTH AMERICA

N THE VICEROYALTY OF Peru, religious art in general, and *relicarios* in particular, evinced a different character from that of New Spain. Although there were similarities, the two Spanish viceroyalties differed widely in terms of geography, culture, history, and, consequently, in artistic expression as well.

In the pre-Columbian era, Mexico and Peru were the two most developed regions in the Western Hemisphere. Their mineral wealth and existing infrastructure made these two regions in the Americas of the most interest to the Spanish. Prior to the Conquest, both were ruled by theocratic oligarchies that had established hegemony over other groups, creating vast empires; both had achieved high levels of civilization and learning.

For a variety of reasons, the development of South America under Spanish rule differed from that in Mesoamerica. A major factor was distance. The lengthy and difficult transport between Spain and her South American colonies, and then the distances between her coastal capital at Lima, established by Francisco Pizarro in 1535, and the important population centers in the rugged mountain highlands, precluded Spain from exerting as tight a control over her colonies in the Viceroyalty of Peru as she did in New Spain. In the late seventeenth century, for example, when the Peruvian chronicler Josephe de Mugaburu and his family traveled from Lima to Cusco for an extended stay, the journey took them fifty days (Mugaburu 1975, 247). By contrast, today Cusco is 357 air miles from Lima, or a flight time of seventy minutes.

In Peru, as in New Spain, the Spanish military and settlers focused their attention on subjugating the Indians and achieving quick gain from gold and silver mines. The laborious tasks of "civilizing" native peoples, proselytizing them, and constructing churches and schools were primarily left to the priests and friars of the principal religious orders: the Augustinians, Dominicans, Franciscans, and Jesuits. The Incan oligarchy, although decimated and robbed of its political power, nevertheless maintained some influence over the native peoples, especially in their ancient capital of Cusco where to this day their language, Quechua, is still spoken intrafamilially by traditional, impoverished Indians as well as by wealthy, affluent intellectuals. The influences of the friars as well as the persistence of Incan culture had major consequences for the artistic development of the Viceroyalty of Peru.

If only because of communication difficulties among Spain, her capital at Lima, and her provincial governments in the Andean mountains, many of the restrictions placed on native artisans in other parts of the Spanish colonies were ineffective in Peru. Consequently, the inclusion of pre-Hispanic religious references and native constructs was evident in architecture, decorative arts, and artisan goods, as it continues to be in the region. Native influences were less discernible in paintings of the early colonial period, however.

At the time of the Conquest, the Incan realm extended from southern Colombia to northern Chile and eastward into the Amazon Basin. Not only was the territory extensive and diverse, it was also rich in minerals. The gold and silver that the Spanish took from the Inca, and the booty they subsequently confiscated from the palaces, tombs, and temples of the Inca, exceeded the value of the riches they had seized in Mexico. But the treasure robbed from the Inca was a trifle when compared to the quantity of precious metals the Spanish extracted from mines throughout the Andes during three hundred years of colonial rule. At Potosí, in present-day Bolivia, using the forced labor of indentured Indians (*mitayos*), the Spanish extracted fabulous riches from what was a veritable mountain of silver (Taullard 1947, 30).

The wealth generated by the Spaniards' mines led to the creation of huge personal fortunes and an opulent, ostentatious colonial life-style in provincial capitals at Potosí, Chuquisaca, Quito, Arequipa, Po-payán, Santa Fé de Bogotá, Cusco, and in the viceregal capital of Lima.

As in New Spain, devotional jewelry was popular in the Viceroy-alty of Peru. Here, too, the wearing of such religious items as *relicarios* was a way for women, and men, to manifest their piety and religious sentiments, display their wealth, and yet avoid offending Crown pro-scriptions against the wearing of sumptuous jewelry.

Relatively few *relicarios* from the colonial period have survived the multiple perils of time, fashion, political chaos, and financial need that too often caused these jewels to be lost or destroyed. The few colonial-period *relicarios* that have survived attest to the excellence of the crafts-manship with which they were created and to the importance they sig-nified to their owners. Although documentation of the manufacture of *relicarios* is scant, inventories, wills, and period portraits demonstrate the popularity these precious lockets once enjoyed among the citizenry of viceregal Peru. Jorge Juan and Antonio de Ulloa described the women of eighteenth-century Panama (governed after 1717 from Lima) as wearing *relicarios* among quantities of gold and coral jewelry around their necks: "They wear five or six chapelets or rows of beads around their necks . . . and besides these one, two or more gold chains, having some relics dependent from them (Juan and De Ulloa 1972, 121)." A 1762 will registered in Cusco describes a sumptuous *relicario*: "Doña Leandra de Lovatón y Costilla, declares that Sra. Costanza Costilla de Valverde y Cartagena, Marquesa de Rocafuerte, in her testament leaves . . . a large gold *relicario* with 107 square cut diamonds, both small and large, with five large pearls and a long chain (Cornejo Bouronde 1960, 305)."

Eighteenth-century *Cartas de Dote*, dowry documents from Ota-valo, a small city in northern Ecuador, frequently mention *relicarios* and indicate that they were most typically of gold and emeralds: in 1745, "a *relicario* with its gold chain and emeralds, appraised at one hundred and fifty pesos" was part of the dowry of Doña Tomasa Chi-riboga, given by her father, the Royal Ensign Don Juan Joseph de Chi-riboga, to his future son-in-law, General Don Manuel de Jijón y León (Lebret 1981, 215).

Some colonial-period *relicarios* were brought from Europe. In 1620 Padre Leonard de Araujo listed *relicarios* among a number of de-

18th-century Altoperuvian *relicario*, oil painting on copper in silver frame, 13.5 cm in diameter, with diamonds and yellow topazes. Obverse: *La Virgen de la Merced*; reverse (not shown): *Ecce Homo*. Photo courtesy of Milagros Gallery, San Antonio, Texas.

votional objects that he transported to Quito from Italy and sold to Doctor Antonio Morga via an intermediary: "six small *relicarios* with their moldings and colorings beneath ovoid glass and with moldings of smooth ebony. . . . A small *relicario* with many relics; a *lámina* within from the hand of de Urbino of the child sleeping with the Virgin San Lorenço; San Juan evangelista molding of smooth ebony (Vargas 1949, 219)." At Doctor Morga's death, the inventory of his goods also included "an illuminated agnus dei enclosed in wood; two large agnus dei framed in silver (Vargas 1949, 225)."

In the Viceroyalty of Peru, as in New Spain, *relicarios* were first and foremost crafted by colonial metalsmiths. These artisans were highly regarded members of colonial society, with their own guilds, chapels, rights to burial within the church, and membership in some of the most prestigious orders of viceregal society (De Lavalle and Lang 1974, 13). Many of the early silversmiths in the Viceroyalty of

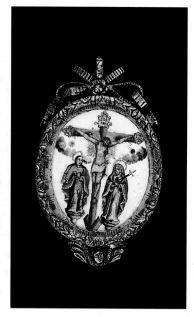

Peru were Flemish-Germans, from the regions of northern Europe then under Spanish dominion. Peter Rudolf, from Dunkirk, and Evan de Amberes (of Antwerp), for example, opened their workshops in Lima in 1550 (De Lavalle and Lang 1974, 14).

Indigenous silversmiths, or those of *color quebrado* (fractured color)—blacks and those of mixed races—were allowed to work as silversmiths, unlike their counterparts in other regions of the Spanish colonial empire. Indian silversmiths were immediately put to work by the Spanish, smelting metal, extracting the royal *quinta*, and making objects for ecclesiastical and personal use. In 1541, when Alonso de Orejuela and Martín de la Calle petitioned the Cabildo of Quito for a license to work silver mines in the region of Tungurahua (central Ecuadoran highlands), they indicated that they would be employing four Indian silversmiths to determine the quality of the extracted metal (Vargas 1982, 91).

Native silversmiths were particularly responsible for the persistence of indigenous forms and motifs in the silverwork of the colonial period, especially in Cusco and the Collao region of highland Peru— Lake Titicaca and its environs (De Lavalle and Lang 1974, 15). Of all

18th-century Ecuadoran *relicario*, 8 × 5 × 1 cm. Carved, polychromed, and gilded ivory in chased and etched gold frame with pearls. Obverse: "The Flight into Egypt"; reverse (not shown): "Saint Sebastian." Museo del Banco Central, Quito, Ecuador. Photo: CH.

Late 18th-century Altoperuvian *relicario*. Oil painting on bone in chased and engraved silver frame, 7.5 × 4.7 × .9 cm. Obverse: *La Coronación de la Virgen de Copacabana*; reverse: *La Virgen y San Juan al Pie de la Cruz.* Private collection. Photo: AR.

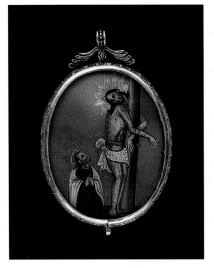 

19th-century Bolivian *relicario*. Oil painting on metal in silver frame, 7.5 × 5 × .7 cm. Obverse: *Cristo a la Columna*; reverse: *La Virgen de Copacabana*. Private collection. Photo: AR.

the artwork produced by native artisans, the most plentiful and coveted works were those produced by Indian gold- and silversmiths (Vargas 1982, 91).

In documents pertaining to the Viceroyalty of Peru, it is rare to find the names of the silversmiths who made *relicarios*, whether large ecclesiastical works or small items for private devotion. Mention has been made of a few. Juan Beltrán, a Jesuit born in Guipúzcoa, Spain, about 1539, who worked at El Escorial and died in Lima at the age of ninety-eight in 1637, was an "illustrious silversmith and in Lima he made many *relicarios* and a frontal that is the best ornament in the church (Vargas Ugarte 1968, 174)." Francisco Mazuelos, presumably a silversmith, received a quantity of gold and silver in 1736 from Father José de la Cruz, the prefect of the Hospital de Moquera (Peru), for San Antonio's monstrance, crown, and lily, as well as *relicarios* and other items, according to the hospital's archives (Vargas Ugarte 1968, 427).

In the Viceroyalty of Peru, and later in the independent republics of the region, *relicario* images were crafted in a variety of materials and techniques. The most popular and skillfully crafted *relicarios* were those created by painters of both academic and folk traditions. Although little known beyond their region's boundaries, the painted *relicarios* of highland South America represent a unique genre of religious miniatures, often of exceptional quality. Images of the Virgin, Christ, and the saints were exquisitely painted on copper, silver, ivory, and mother-of-pearl, sometimes with a single horsehair, by unknown artists whose detailing is best appreciated when examined under a magnifying lens.

In the Andes, the art of miniature painting that was to reach a high point in the late nineteenth century began in the early colonial period with illuminists trained in Italy and Spain. According to the Colombian art historian Gabriel Giraldo Jaramillo, "the miniature portrait gradually replaces the art of the decorators and illuminators of books who bit by bit are disappearing (Giraldo Jaramillo 1982, 11)."

One of the earliest teachers of the art of illumination in South America may have been Fray Pedro Gocial, a Flemish Franciscan born about 1497 and active as a painter in Quito between 1534 and 1557. Fray Pedro also directed the art school at the Colegio of San Andrés in Quito, founded in 1552 by Franciscans Fray Jodoco Ricke and Fray Francisco de Morales to train Indians and mestizos in the arts and trades (Vargas 1949, 158). Documents of the mid-sixteenth century indicate that Fray Pedro was an influential miniaturist whose students were well trained and considered "very perfect painters and scribes and record keepers (Vargas 1949, 106)."

Among the first native-born Americans to learn and teach the illuminists' art in the Andes was Fray Pedro Bedón, a Dominican born in Quito in 1556 of a Spanish father and Creole mother. Bedón studied in Lima with one of the most important artists of the colonial period in Peru, the Spanish painter Mateo Pérez de Alesio (Angulo Íñiguez 1950, 467). Mateo Pérez de Alesio's son, Fray Adriano de Alesio, a Dominican born in Lima, also learned the art of illumination in his father's workshop, which functioned as an art school in the Peruvian capital (Vargas Ugarte 1968, 128).

In 1599 Capitán Pedro de Reynalte Coello, the son of Alonso Sánchez Coello, Spain's most important portrait painter at the court of Felipe II, resided in Callao, Lima's port (Vargas Ugarte 1968, 330). He served as a military aide to the viceroy but was also known as an excellent illuminist painter and portraitist (Angulo Íñiguez 1950, 476). He is especially remembered for his portrait of San Francisco Solano, painted thirty-six hours after the saint's death (Vargas Ugarte 1968, 330). It is possible that Coello, like his father, painted miniature portraits as well.

19th-century Bolivian *relicario*. Oil painting on metal in silver frame, 8.5 × 6.2 × .7 cm. Obverse: *La Virgen de Pomata*; reverse: *Al Pie de la Cruz* (At the Foot of the Cross). Private collection. Photo: AR.

Also in 1599, Fray Diego de Ocaña, one of the most important artists of the seventeenth century in Viceregal Peru, arrived in Lima from Panama. A native of Toledo, Spain, Fray Ocaña became a Jeronymite friar and lived at the Monasterio de Guadalupe in Extremadura before being sent to Peru by his superiors. The style of his drawings and paintings indicates that Ocaña was trained as an illuminist. His work was to exert a major influence on Andean painting, including the painting of *relicarios*. His most celebrated painting is of the Virgin of Guadalupe, after the image of the same name in his Spanish monastery (as distinct from the image in Tepeyac, Mexico). Ocaña painted his Virgin on wood for the church at Chuquisaca, present-day Sucre, Bolivia. Later, the painting was decorated with silver and gold at the request of the faithful, who also covered her image in jewels, some of them quite valuable (Gisbert 1987, 8). The faces of the dark-skinned Virgin and the child she is holding peer out from a dazzling, flat, patterned metallic surface with the frontal communication of a Byzantine icon. This work, and others like it left by Ocaña in his sojourn through Altoperu, was widely replicated by other painters, especially Gregorio Gamarra (De Mesa and Gisbert 1977, 38). Into the twentieth century, folk painters of *latitas* (tin *retablos*) and *relicarios* continued to paint and gild iconlike virgins with the same archaic qualities as those of Ocaña's Virgin of Guadalupe.

In the northern regions of the Viceroyalty of Peru, in the province of Nueva Granada (present-day Colombia, Venezuela, Panama, and Ecuador), illuminist painters also painted *relicarios* and developed a separate school of miniature painting during the colonial period. Although they originally exercised their craft by illuminating religious books and documents, these artists also appear to have painted *relicarios*. In 1607 a Peruvian Indian, Bartolomé de Figueroa, opened a school for Indian painters (Giraldo Jaramillo 1948, 41). One of his pupils was Gregorio Vásquez de Arce y Ceballos, a prolific painter of large-scale works on canvas who also painted miniatures in oils on shell, wood, canvas, and copper plates (Giraldo Jaramillo 1982, 21). His biographer, José Manuel Groot, himself an accomplished miniaturist, wrote in 1859 of Vásquez's work: "It is difficult to believe that one who works as a painter of large canvases also paints tiny figures with such perfection. I have seen a *relicario* two inches long, with a bust of San Ignacio on one side and on the reverse a full portrait of the seated Virgin, painted in oil on a sheet of copper with a gold frame

(Giraldo Jaramillo 1982, 21)." Vásquez's daughter, Feliciana, also painted religious miniatures in her father's style (Giraldo Jaramillo 1982, 23).

Another Figueroa disciple, Tomás Fernández de Heredia, painted religious miniatures. At least two signed works of his survive, both dated 1676. These paintings, depicting a Holy Martyr with the Trinity, are in the Museo Colonial of Bogotá. Giraldo Jaramillo describes them as being "of such small dimensions that they can be considered true miniatures, that show his great drawing and colorist abilities (Giraldo Jaramillo 1948, 114)."

One of the most accomplished miniaturists of the eighteenth century, and an important artist of the Quito school, was the Ecuadoran Indian nun Madre Magdalena Dávalos, a disciple of the sculptor Bernardo Legarda. Madre Magdalena, who entered the Carmelite order in Quito in 1742 (Vargas 1949, 57), was a talented musician and sculptor of religious images as well as a painter of exquisite miniatures (Giraldo Jaramillo 1982, 17).

Her compatriot, Manuel Samaniego y Jaramillo, born in Quito about 1767, was one of the most prolific and influential painters of the colonial period in the Andes. Vargas Ugarte called him a "competent miniaturist of religious themes (Vargas Ugarte 1968, 460)." In addition to his large works on canvas, Samaniego painted miniatures of popular religious subjects such as Our Lady of Mercy, the Divine Shepherdess, and the Inmaculada for a public that solicited his work from Lima, Guayaquil, Bogotá, and elsewhere (Vargas 1949, 135).

Although many illuminists painted religious miniatures such as *relicarios*, certainly all did not. In the eighteenth and early nineteenth centuries, some Andean miniaturists lent their talents to producing exquisitely detailed drawings of plants and flowers, most notably for the botanical expeditions organized by the Spanish naturalist José Celestino Mutis, who arrived in Nueva Granada in 1760, and Baron Alexander von Humboldt, who explored South America for five years beginning in 1799. The fine details of flora and fauna that are sometimes evident in nineteenth-century South American *relicarios* are a legacy from the botanical painters of the late colonial period.

The painting of religious miniatures for *relicarios* was an activity of workshops and professional painters who were primarily engaged in the production of large works for the church, government, and private patrons. As in Europe and in New Spain, many painters and sculptors

19th-century Bolivian *relicario*. Oil painting on silver in silver frame, 8.5 × 6 × .8 cm. Obverse: *La Coronación de la Virgen*; reverse (not shown): *La Virgen de Copacabana*. Private collection. Photo: AR.

of Viceroyal Peru, including some of the finest painters of the day, created religious miniatures as a sideline to their regular work, but because *relicarios* were almost always unsigned and unrecorded, it is difficult, if not impossible, to attribute with certainty the painting of a specific *relicario* to a particular painter.

All of the painters of *relicarios*, however, whether trained as illuminists or painters or artistically untrained, were greatly influenced by the styles and conceits of the principal schools of Andean painting—those of Quito (Ecuador), Cusco (Peru), and Potosí (Bolivia).

In Altoperu, present-day Peru and Bolivia, the prolific schools of

19th-century Bolivian *relicario*. Oil painting on metal in silver frame, 11.5 × 9 × .8 cm. Obverse: "*La Virgen de Guadalupe*" (Sucre, Bolivia, after the Diego de Ocaña painting); reverse (not shown): "*San Gabriel Arcángel*." Private collection. Photo: AR.

painting of colonial Cusco and Potosí produced a number of artists who painted *relicarios*. During the sixteenth century the output of painters' workshops was strictly controlled by Flemish, Italian, and Spanish masters and their disciples, who stressed rigid conformity to European standards and ecclesiastical dictates.

By the seventeenth century, however, Indian and mestizo painters in Altoperu were beginning to develop their own vernacular, adapting European constructs to their own tastes. The school of religious painting that evolved during the seventeenth and eighteenth centuries in Cusco, and by extension in Potosí, is characterized by a distinctive folk style, one that reflects a native perspective: "The faces and the bodies of their saints are Andean faces and bodies. The Virgins are *cholas* [native women], and the bearded Santiagos, Isidros or Cristos are Indians who have mestizo characteristics (Macera 1979, xlv)." The compositions are hieratic, allegorical, and narrative, with unidimensional and frontal figures. The virgins are dressed as dolls or as Incan princesses (*ñustas*). Symbols important to the Andean Indian people are emphasized: the sun, the moon, and the *kantuta* flower.

The lavish use of gold, the mystical, magical reflection of the sun, is a manifestation of what André Emmerich calls the Peruvians' "sheetmetal aesthetic (Emmerich 1984, xxii)." It is one of the most noteworthy aspects of Altoperuvian popular painting, including the painting of *relicarios*. Intricate gold tracery, reminiscent of Cordovan leather tooling, decorates the garments of these virgins, sometimes to a dazzling effect. The nearly solid gold surface of a painting is interrupted only by the solemn brown faces of the Indian mother and child as they confront the viewer from openings in the golden expanses of their rigid, embossed garments.

The themes of Andean religious folk painting were adapted to native tastes as well. Armed soldier angels replaced minor deities; Illapa, the god of thunder and lightning, became Santiago, the soldier saint; and the most important celestial personage for the Andean people, Pachamama, the Earth Mother, became the Virgin, a somber Indian mother standing stiffly with her child. The iconlike quality of the numerous virgins venerated throughout the Andean highlands has frequently been noted by art historians: "If they have a Byzantine rigidity, this is mitigated by a native gracefulness; the lack of a tactile quality is dissimulated by the floral decoration that fills the space with arabesque altars," writes Cossio del Pomar (1929, 211).

A number of art historians have commented on the Byzantine look to Andean folk painting, specifically in the depictions of the regional virgins. The aesthetic that led Indian and mestizo painters to produce these unidimensional, frontal figures shimmering in gold may simply be a coincidence between native South American and Byzantine tastes. The influence of Italian Mannerists trained in Rome, in all likelihood, contributed to the genre. Mateo Pérez de Alesio, the Jesuit Bernardo Bitti, and Angelino Medoro were all instrumental in training native painters in early colonial Peru, as was the Spanish gilder Pedro de Vargas, an accomplished miniaturist famed for his

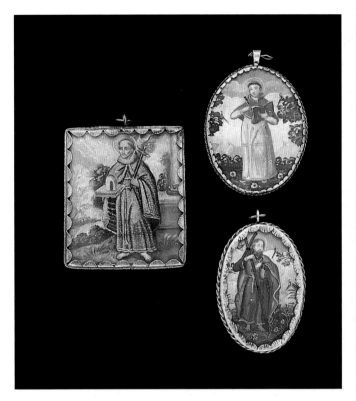

enamel-like paintings on copper. The works of these artists and their disciples, housed in the churches of the Altoperuvian highlands, would inspire local folk painters for centuries.

Martín Soria, however, suggests a direct influence from Byzantium on the painters of Altoperuvian virgins. He says that icons produced by Cretan madonna painters active in Venice in the sixteenth century reached the Andes and that a number of these icons—virgins with gold sprinkled liberally over their stiff garments—survive in Spain and in South America, where they have been mistaken for Spanish colonial work (Kubler and Soria 1959, 324).

By the early eighteenth century the most remarkable school of painting in Spain's American colonies had evolved in the ancient Inca capital of Cusco. The fame of this school of exuberant religious painting, much of it produced by anonymous mestizo and Indian craftsmen, spread far and wide. Fueled by the colonists' demand for such luxuries

18th-century Altoperuvian *relicarios*, possibly from the Cusco area. Oil painting on copper in silver frames, the largest of which is 9.5 × 7.5 × .8 cm. Obverse, from left to right: *San Pedro Alcántara*, *San Ramón Nonato* (?), and *San Andrés*; reverse, from left to right: *La Inmaculada Concepción*, *La Virgen de la Candelaria*, and *La Inmaculada Concepción*. Private collection. Photo: AR.

19th-century Bolivian *relicario*. Oil painting on metal in silver frame, 19 × 13 × 1.3 cm. Obverse: *La Virgen del Socavón*; reverse: *Cristo de la Paciencia*. Private collection. Photo: AR.

as artworks, Cusco workshops produced religious paintings in nearly industrial quantities by the mid-eighteenth century. Orders for canvases came from convents, churches, institutions, and individuals from as far away as Tucumán (northwest Argentina), Trujillo, on the north coast of Peru, and Santiago, Chile, to the south.

The Cusco school exerted a lasting effect on the folk art of the southern Andean highlands, yet perhaps the artists of the Potosí school had a greater and more direct impact on the painting of nineteenth-century *relicario* images. Popular-style religious art from Potosí differed from that of Cusco in its more marked primitive style. Soria describes the Potosí images as being flatter and more angular; and gold is applied in a spotted pattern rather than continuously, as in the Cusco style (Kubler and Soria 1959, 327).

In Potosí, at one time the most affluent community in the Spanish colonies, a heavy output of mass-produced art responded to wealthy Spanish and mestizo colonists' demands for religious works, as had been the case in Cusco, but Potosino painters were also employed in filling orders from the *mitayos*—conscripted Indians forced to work in the silver mines for a fixed period of time, who were brought to Potosí by the thousands from villages all over the highlands, especially the Collao region—Lake Titicaca and its environs. In Potosí they worked under dreadful conditions that many did not survive. The *mitayos* were homesick for the familiar images of their local virgins and saints, painted by village artisans in typically Indian style with heavy use of gold overlays, hierarchical composition, and the inclusion of angels, flowers, tiny animals, birds, and people. Because the Indians sought religious works for devotional purposes, these paintings served utilitarian as much as aesthetic needs and were often crudely executed. Yet the religious art produced in Potosí for an Indian public was nonetheless compelling. The abundant folk depictions of the Virgin of Copacabana, the Virgin of Pomata, Santiago, San Miguel, the angels with arquebuses, and other subjects were popular not only among the native population. They also exerted an influence on the work of the better painters of Potosí, among them Melchor Pérez Holguín (1660–1724), who painted his Virgen de la Leche against a backdrop of gold (De Mesa 1988, 14).

While the folk painters of Potosí produced works for the poorer classes, Indian leaders of the *mitayos* became some of the most important patrons of the more skilled Potosí painters. The work of Gaspar Miguel de Berrio (active 1730–1758), a student of Holguín, shows strong Indian influences, as does that of his contemporary, the Indian painter and sculptor Luis Niño. These painters in turn exerted an important influence on the folk painters and folk artists of the nineteenth and twentieth centuries in highland Peru and Bolivia. Berrio and Luis Niño are thought to have painted *latitas* and may have painted *relicarios* as well. Their pupils certainly were responsible for such work. Even into the twentieth century, Indian folk painters working in the colonial Potosí style continued to produce popular religious paintings for a traditional public of Indians and mestizos (Otero 1958, 388).

Many *relicarios* were painted in Potosí during the colonial period. The production of these miniatures was lucrative and much in demand (Otero 1958, 387). Most typical were popular images of the Virgin, the saints, Christ, and angels painted on ovals of silver sheet and encased behind glass in silver, gold, or filigree frames.

Throughout the colonial period, *relicarios* produced in Potosí and other regions of the Andes were in wide use within the cloistered walls of the convents of Viceregal Peru. They were worn by nuns as badges of hagiographical affiliation, similar in use (though smaller) to the *escudos de monja* worn by the Conceptionist and Jeronymite nuns of New Spain. The saint or saints to whom a nun was particularly devoted were depicted, along with the image of the particular virgin to whom her convent was dedicated (De Mesa and Gisbert 1990, 8).

In Altoperu, *relicarios* were also worn by laypersons, members of Third Orders, the military and their families, and visitors to certain

19th-century Bolivian *relicario*. Oil painting on metal in silver frame, 10.5 × 8 × .8 cm. Obverse: *San Gabriel*; reverse (not shown): *La Virgen del Socavón*. Private collection. Photo: AR.

19th-century Bolivian *relicario*. Oil painting on metal in silver frame, 13.7 × 10 × .8 cm. Obverse: *San Honofre* (the iconography is confused with that of *San Jerónimo*); reverse (not shown): *La Virgen del Socavón*. Private collection. Photo: AR.

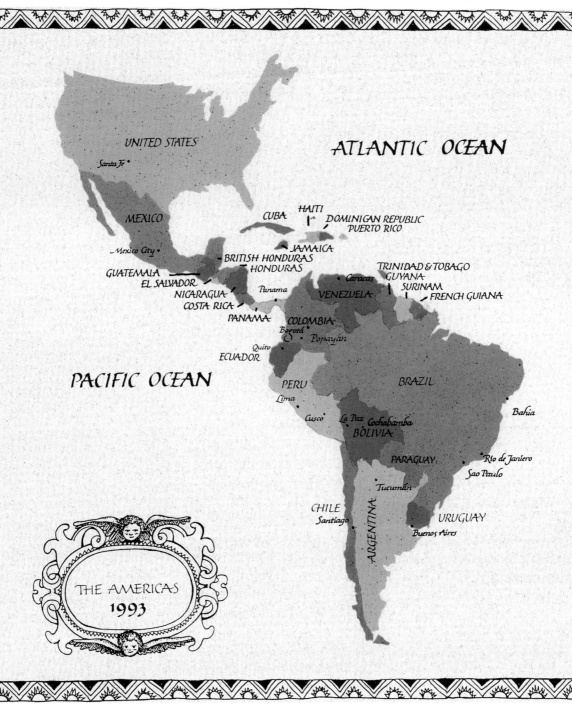

UNITED STATES

Santa Fe

ATLANTIC OCEAN

MEXICO

Mexico City

CUBA   HAITI

DOMINICAN REPUBLIC
PUERTO RICO

JAMAICA

BRITISH HONDURAS
HONDURAS

GUATEMALA
EL SALVADOR

TRINIDAD & TOBAGO
GUYANA

Caracas   SURINAM

NICARAGUA
COSTA RICA

Panama

VENEZUELA   FRENCH GUIANA

PANAMA

COLOMBIA

Bogotá

Popayán

Quito
ECUADOR

PACIFIC OCEAN

PERU   BRAZIL

Lima

Bahia

Cusco   *La Paz* *Cochabamba*

BOLIVIA

PARAGUAY   *Río de Janiero*

Sao Paulo

Tucumán

CHILE

Santiago

ARGENTINA

URUGUAY

Buenos Aires

THE AMERICAS
1993

pilgrimage sites. *Relicarios* worn by the laity were often much smaller than those worn by nuns. As in New Spain, *relicarios* served the devout of Viceregal Peru as protection and for inspiration. They were hung on or near the image of a favorite saint as a votive offering and graced the walls of homes and dormitories.

In the nineteenth century, *relicarios* became one of the most noteworthy artistic expressions in the Andes, reaching a high point of development before disappearing altogether. Even in the midst of the terrible political upheavals that beset Spain's former colonies in the Americas, the folk arts experienced a genesis, rise, and fall everywhere in Hispanic Latin America. Kubler maintains that the brief disappearance of the Spaniards' methods of agrarian exploitation left rural people with an unused surplus of time and energy that had previously been absorbed by the landlords and tax farmers. People found themselves free to create things for their own pleasure and use, until toward the end of the century when the new tyranny of the industrial revolution again made demands on their time and energies. "Folk art occupies the brief interlude between court taste and commercial taste," Kubler states (1964, 5). In the remote rural areas of the Andes, where a barter economy prevailed into at least the mid-twentieth century, the folk art phenomenon, including the painting of *relicarios*, lasted much longer than it did in urban areas.

Relicarios, called *medallones* by some in the region, were most commonly paintings of religious themes on plates of copper, silver, zinc, or other metals in circular, elliptical, octagonal, or rectangular form. *Relicarios* from central and northern Peru are often rectangular while those of the Potosí region are characteristically elliptical. Nineteenth-century Andean *relicarios* rarely contained actual relics of the saints; the designation had become completely symbolical by the end of the colonial era. Most Andean *relicarios* contain paintings on two separate surfaces encased in the locket. Sometimes, however, the sheet of copper or silver has been painted on both sides with *relicario* images. Painting on other surfaces such as bone, ivory, paper, and vellum was less common in the southern Andes than was painting on metal.

Toward the end of the nineteenth century, *nacar* (mother-of-pearl) became a favorite surface for the painting of *relicarios*. These *relicarios* are particularly associated with the pilgrimage site to Our Lady of Copacabana on the shores of Lake Titicaca. Some of these

Bolivian *relicario* of the Coronation of Our Lady of Copacabana, painted in oils on an oyster shell that has been surrounded in chased silver with a chased and engraved finial; a thin border of reverse painting on glass frames the shell. The interior is inscribed: "*A devoción de Emilia Cueto, octubre 5 de 1907.*" Dimensions: 10.6 × 5.5 × 3 cm.

19th-century Bolivian *relicario*, oil painting on mother-of-pearl in frame of chased and engraved 22 k. gold, with a border of reverse painting on the glass covering the medallion. Obverse: the Virgin of Copacabana; reverse: Our Lady of Carmel. Private collection. Photo: AR.

Late 19th- to early 20th-century Bolivian *relicario*. Oil on mother-of-pearl in gold frame, 1.5 × 2 cm. Obverse (not shown): La Virgen de Copapcabana; reverse: La Virgen Inmaculada with angels and four saints. Private collection. Photo: AR.

miniatures were of exceptionally fine painting and detail and were said to have been painted with a single horsehair. Many were quite small—thumbnail size—although often an entire religious scene was painted on them. These smaller *relicarios* were hung from rosaries, watches, necklaces, and *bastones de manda* (authorities' canes) and continued to be made in highland Bolivia into the twentieth century, when they were replaced by cheap imported trinkets (Gisbert 1990, 26).

Although exquisite lockets of gold and silver were sometimes crafted by master silversmiths throughout the nineteenth century, most of the *relicario* lockets of the post-Independence period were simple two-sided frames of silver or gold, perhaps with a rope of twisted metal encircling the locket as added decoration. Smooth or toothed edges held glass over the paintings on each side of the frame, and a ring at the top of the locket provided for suspension of the *relicario* (De Mesa and Gisbert 1990, 13).

It appears that the bulk of the finely painted *relicarios* made in highland Peru and Bolivia between 1825 and the end of the nineteenth century were the work of a relatively few painters and were most commonly purchased at popular pilgrimage sites such as Our Lady of Copacabana and the Sanctuary to the Virgin of Guadalupe in Sucre, Bolivia.

The Franciscan chronicler of the history of the *santuario* at Copacabana, Fray P. Fernando de M. Sanjinés, writing in 1909, described the popularity of *relicarios* at the popular pilgrimage site: "And who among them [the pilgrims] doesn't have at least a medal, or they obtain a *relicario*, a medallion of her image [Our Lady of Copacabana], to fasten to one's chest as a powerful talisman? Everyone, the greatest and the most humble, all want to take home with them some souvenir, before departing from the traditional pilgrimage (Sanjinés 1909, 125)."

Relicarios from Copacabana have been found far and wide. The gold-framed *relicario* shown here, with the Virgin of Copacabana painted on one side of the mother-of-pearl surface and the Virgen del Carmen on the reverse, was for generations a prized possession of the Osorio family, prominent sugarcane growers in the Philippines, who sold it to an American collector some years ago.

Relicario medallions that bear the name of their *donante* (donor) or depict the person, usually kneeling at the Virgin's feet, were sometimes votive offerings given to a favorite image. Such personalized *reli-*

Bolivian *relicario*. Oil painting on metal with reverse painted glass border in silver frame, 13.5 × 8.7 × 1 cm. Obverse: the Virgin of Copacabana and the inscription "Viva Bolivia! May the Virgin protect Don José Ballivián" (the fourth president of Bolivia). The moon beneath the Virgin's feet reads "Our Lady of the Stars 1832." On the reverse is the image of Our Lady of Carmel with the Bolivian flag. The inscription reads, "And Doña Mercedes Coll as well" (General Ballivián's wife).

19th-century Bolivian *relicario*. Oil painting on metal in silver frame, 13.7 × 10 × .8 cm. Obverse: *La Virgen del Socavón*, depicted with soldiers and flags of the emerging states of Peru and Bolivia; reverse (page 87): *San Honofre*. Private collection. Photo: AR.

carios were also worn as protection by travelers or soldiers going into battle. A famous example of the latter can be seen here. General José Ballivián, fourth president of Bolivia and hero of the Battle of Ingavi in 1841, is said to have worn this *relicario* into the battle.

The subjects depicted in the nineteenth-century *relicarios* of the southern highlands of Peru and Bolivia were relatively limited. The most popular are the virgins: La Virgen de Copacabana, after the original image sculpted by Francisco Tupac Yupanqui in 1583; La Virgen del Carmen, patron saint of soldiers; La Virgen del Socavón de Oruro, beloved of soldiers as well as miners; Nuestra Señora la Bella de Arani (Cochabamba); La Virgen de Guadalupe de Chuquisaca (Sucre), after the seventeenth-century painting by Diego de Ocaña; La Virgen de Pomata; La Virgen de la Paz with the Holy Trinity; and others. Many of the *relicarios* painted in the first half of the nineteenth century depict the virgins against a backdrop of flags of the emerging states—the red and white flag of Peru or the red, yellow, and green flag of Bolivia. Some have *donantes* at their feet, some are identified, and sometimes these *relicarios* are dated.

Christ is a popular subject and is depicted mostly in penitential attitudes: Cristo al Pilar, El Señor de la Caña, Cristo Crucificado, El Señor de la Sentencia, and others.

The list of saints in Altoperuvian *relicarios* is somewhat limited: female saints such as Santa Rosa de Lima, Santa Teresa de Ávila, Santa Rita, Santa Bárbara, and others appear; and male saints such as San Miguel Arcángel, San José with the Christ child, San Francisco de Paulo, San Ignacio, San Antonio, San Nicolás de Bari, Santiago Matamoros, and others are found.

The names of some nineteenth-century *latita* painters are known, and it is thought that these folk artists and members of their circles painted *relicarios* as well: Joaquin Castañón, whose painting dates from 1855; Juan de la Cruz Tapia, the most important painter in Potosí in the nineteenth century; Manuel Pereira, who signed a "Virgen de la Candelaria" on tin in 1872; and a painter whom José de Mesa and Teresa Gisbert have named the "Maestro de Arani" (De Mesa and Gisbert 1990, 10).

By the end of the nineteenth century in the highlands of Peru and Bolivia, the painting of *relicarios* had for the most part become a lost art. The introduction of photography in 1856 in Bolivia (Gisbert 1990, 28) and the proliferation of inexpensive colored prints in the second

19th-century Ecuadoran *relicario*. Oil painting on paper in carved wood frame, 11 × 9.7 cm. In the center is an image of *San José con el Niño*. Encircling the image are ten miniature medallions depicting *Santa Inés*, *Santa Bárbara*, *Santa Agueda*, and other female martyrs. On the reverse are tiny relics and *filactería*—strips of paper identifying the relics. Museo de Arte Colonial, Quito. (detail) *Santa Inés*, oil on paper in wood frame. The image is 1.1 × .9 cm. Photo: CH.

half of the nineteenth century, as well as changing popular tastes, sounded a death knell for the patient art of painting *relicarios* in the southern Andean highlands.

In northern South America, the art of painting *relicarios* followed a somewhat different evolution from that of the genre in the highlands of Peru and Bolivia following independence from Spain. Particularly in Colombia, the art of painting portrait miniatures became one of the most popular artistic expressions of the post-Independence period. Artists, both professionals and amateurs, painted delicate images of saints as well as portraits of loved ones and of classical imagery that were treasured in lockets and worn as jewelry.

Giraldo Jaramillo attributes the popularity of miniature portraits, medallions, and cameos in Colombia to the romanticism of the age (Giraldo Jaramillo 1948, 105). Art of the republican era, although technically inferior to that of the colonial period, was spontaneous, ingenuous, human, and reflective of the time, place, and values of the society for which it was produced. Colonial-period canvases of Nueva Granada, by comparison, related little or nothing of the people and period.

In Colombia, as elsewhere in Latin America, religious art went into a great decline in the republican period, yet nearly all of the Colombian miniature painters of this era painted *relicarios*, often of exceptionally fine quality. Many of the finest Colombian miniaturists

18th-century Ecuadoran *relicario*. Oil painting on bone in silver frame, 4.2 × 3.2 × .6 cm. *La Virgen de la Silla/* Seated Madonna. Museo de Arte Colonial, Quito, Ecuador. Photo: CH.

18th–19th-century Peruvian *relicario*. High-relief carved, polychromed, and gilded *piedra huamanga* medallion in gold frame, 10 cm in length. *La Virgen del Carmen*. Private collection. Photo: AR.

were women. Rosa Groot and her sister Dolores, daughters of the well-known painter José Manuel Groot (1800–1878), followed their father's profession (Giraldo Jaramillo 1948, 98). The Groot sisters often painted on ivory, which had been introduced into Colombia in the mid-eighteenth century. Perhaps the most important personage in the nineteenth-century art world in Colombia was Ramón Torres Méndez (1809–1885), who painted more than one hundred miniatures on ivory. His daughters Clementina, Adelaida, and Abelina, as well as a son, Francisco, all followed their father in his trade (Giraldo Jaramillo 1982, 115).

While the most abundant and easily recognized *relicarios* of Spanish-speaking South America are the Altoperuvian paintings on metal or mother-of-pearl, with their distinctive style of gilded and well-painted folk imagery, other types of *relicario* images were also crafted in South America during the colonial period and into the early twentieth century. In the Viceroyalty of Peru, as in New Spain, *relicario* images were sculpted as well as painted in a variety of materials. In the early colonial period such materials as boxwood, orangewood, and ivory were used for the crafting of *relicarios*, either as three-dimensional images or as bas-relief medallions. This work was rarely as finely carved as that of New Spain, however.

One of the unique materials used in the former Viceroyalty of

Peru for the sculpting of *relicarios* was the native Peruvian alabaster known as *piedra de huamanga*, or Huamanga stone. Rubén de la Borbolla, former director of the Museum of Popular Art in Mexico City and an authority on Latin American folk art, has called the Peruvian alabaster carvings one of the most interesting folk-art expressions in the Americas (De Lavalle and Lang 1980, 10). Huamanga stone *relicarios* are most commonly associated with the central and southern highlands of Peru.

The carving of Peruvian alabaster is an ancient practice. Long before the arrival of the Spanish, the Indians of highland Peru made and treasured amulets carved of *piedra de huamanga* most commonly called *illas* or *rumi chacra* by Quechua speakers and *mullu* by the Aymaras. Father Bernabé Cobo, a Spanish Jesuit writing in 1626, described the natives' alabaster carvings: "In the diocese of Guamanga there is a large hill full of veins of a fine alabaster white as snow, of which small images are carved, very curious ones that are appreciated wherever they might be taken (Stastny 1971, 167)."

Bas-relief medallions and sometimes small three-dimensional images were carved for *relicarios* in *huamanga* stone on one or both sides in a variety of sizes, then either coated with wax to preserve the whiteness of the alabaster or lightly polychromed for additional decoration and detail; sometimes the alabaster was gilded as well. In traditional *relicario* fashion, these medallions or tiny images were set behind glass in silver or gold lockets and suspended from chains, *rosario* necklaces, or ribbons.

Another regional style of bas-relief *relicarios* appeared in northwest Argentina, in the provinces of Jujuy, Salta, and Tucumán. Because of a scarcity of hardwoods in these arid areas, artisans for centuries have used a homemade plaster-based *pasta* to craft *relicario* medallions and figures. Village artisans throughout South America have used this inexpensive and easily manufactured material to sculpt religious imagery and decorative elements for chapels. While the exact composition of an artisan's *pasta* is often a carefully guarded secret, the primary ingredient is plaster. Flour, mashed potatoes, glue, fruit juice, cactus sap, and other items are added to the plaster to make the *pasta* elastic and malleable when wet yet hard and durable when dried.

The *pasta relicarios* of northwestern Argentina are mold-made bas-relief plaques or tiny, crude *santos* set in frames of silver, tin, or other metals. Additional decoration is added to the image with paint

18th–19th-century Peruvian *relicario*. Bas-relief carved and polychromed *piedra huamanga* medallion in engraved silver frame, 6.5 × 4.5 × 2 cm. Obverse: *La Virgen del Carmen*; reverse: *San Francisco Javier*. Private collection. Photo: AR.

19th-century *relicario* from northwest Argentina. Sculpted and polychromed *pasta* medallion in silver frame, 5 cm high. Obverse: *La Virgen del Luján*; reverse: *La Coronación de la Virgen*. Palace of the Governors, Museum of New Mexico, Santa Fe. Photo: AR.

and sometimes gilding as well. In the nineteenth century, the makers of these molded images were Colla Indians or others from the highland regions of present-day Bolivia, who were said to have practiced their art for centuries. The inclusion of these crude images in an old Indian grave of the region indicates that this devotional art has been practiced for some time (Onelli 1916, 14). In a monograph published in 1916, the Argentinian scholar Clemente Onelli described his encounter with one of the sellers of these *relicarios*, which he also called *medallones* or *tecas* (from the Greek "theca," meaning "religious medallion"). "The medallion . . . acquired in Tucumán, and which represents San Antonio, I bought for fifty cents. The person who traded me for it (the word "trade" being sacred among these dealers in holy images) claimed that only he could make this image, and that in addition to the great amount of work it cost him to bend the piece of tin and varnish it as a receptacle, for the glass he had had to purchase in the city lenses from discarded eyeglasses (Onelli 1916, 14)."

In Colombia and Ecuador, tagua nut was used for the carving of *relicario* images. This palm nut, grown commercially along the western coast of South America, is also known as vegetable ivory or ivory nut. It is exported primarily to Europe, where it is used for the manufacture of buttons. When soft, it is easy to carve, but then it hardens to an ivorylike durability. Because of its small size, usually 5 to 8 cm long, its use by sculptors is limited to miniatures. During the colonial era in northwestern South America, skilled artisans employed tagua for the carving of diminutive images: tiny *santos*; miniature nativity scenes; hands, heads, and feet for wooden *santos*; and *relicario* plaques and medallions. The material was an inexpensive and handy substitute for ivory, which was highly prized but expensive and rare in South America. As a sculptural medium, vegetable ivory was treated in much the same way as true ivory; tagua carvings were also polychromed and gilded for additional detail and ornamentation. The material ages in much the same way that ivory does, achieving a darkened patina with years of handling and exposure to candle smoke. Tagua-nut *relicarios* are most typically a product of eighteenth-century workshops in Quito.

By the late nineteenth century in the republics that had formerly comprised the Viceroyalty of Peru, *relicarios* were a much degenerated form of devotional art. The finely painted or sculpted *relicario* images in their silver or gold casings were replaced by inexpensive mass-

18th-century Ecuadoran *relicario*. Two-sided bas-relief tagua nut medallion in silver frame. Obverse: *La Trinidad*; reverse: *San Lorenzo*. Museo Municipal Alberto Mena Caamaño, Quito. Photo: CH.

produced chromolithographs, photographic prints, or even photocopied images of favorite virgins, Christ, and the saints in lockets of inexpensive base metal. The "glass" protecting the image might be a sheet of clear plastic or the concave lens from a discarded pair of eyeglasses.

In twentieth-century South America, as in Mexico and Guatemala, the use of *relicarios* was most persistent among Indians living in remote regions. In the highlands of southern Colombia and northern Ecuador, for example, Indian women continue into the present era to wear *relicarios* as pendants from their traditional coral or red-bead *rosario* necklaces. The *relicario* lockets worn by these Quichua speakers resemble watch casings. They are generally circular and approximately 5 to 8 cm in diameter. Sometimes they are made of silver but most are of a silver- or gold-colored base metal. The lockets usually contain a

18th-century Ecuadoran *relicario*. Carved and polychromed bas-relief medallion of tagua nut in laminated and gilded-silver filigree frame, 6×5×1 cm. Obverse: *La Virgen Eucarística*; reverse (not shown): *San Antonio de Padua*. Banco Central del Ecuador, Quito. Photo: CH.

Mid-20th-century northern Ecuadoran *relicarios*. Left: religious print of *San Lázaro* in silver frame, 7.6×6.2 cm, on necklace of brass and red glass trade beads. Right: a similar *relicario*, 8.6×7 cm, etched silver with a print of the Child Jesus on the reverse. Courtesy: Que Tenga Buena Mano, Santa Fe, New Mexico. Photo: AR.

relicario image only on one side, typically a religious print protected by a sheet of glass. The reverse side of the locket might be decorated with a floral design, a cross, or a sacred heart etched in the metal. Three small concave dangles, called *pailas* (miniatures of cooking pans), hang from the sides and bottom of the *relicario* while a ring at the top provides for suspension of the locket from a necklace, ribbon, or chain.

In certain regions of highland South America, as well as in Mexico and Guatemala, traditional Indians have used *relicarios* as decorative and symbolical elements in the elaborate dance costumes of Indian festivals since at least the mid-nineteenth century, and their use continues into present times.

In the Ecuadoran highlands south of Quito, for example, *relicarios* are important components in the elaborate headdresses—*umas*—worn by dancers in the festival of Corpus Christi. Either the hoop or nine-pointed star-shaped headdress—depending upon the village of origin—is decorated with all manner of beads, mirrors, discarded jewelry, coins, plastic babies, stylized lambs, and devotional objects such as crosses, medals, and *relicarios*. The use of coins, mirrors, and *relicarios*, all of them flat, shiny, reflective surfaces, recalls the pre-

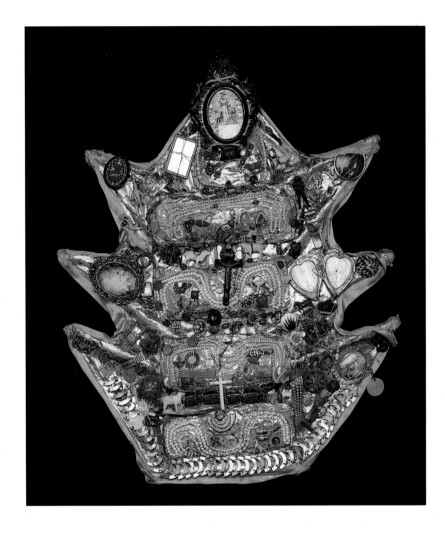

Mid-20th century *uma*—dance headdress for *Corpus Cristi* festival in the central highlands of Ecuador, Cotopaxi province. Dimensions are 86.1 × 70 × 8.3 cm. Gold paper, plastic animals, costume jewelry, mirrors, *relicarios*, and other symbolical and decorative objects cover a bentwood frame. International Folk Art Collections at the Museum of International Folk Art, Santa Fe, New Mexico. Photo: AR.

Hispanic use of shiny silver and gold plaques that decorated ceremonial garb. Chroniclers describe these costumes and the dazzling effect they had on viewers.

The artisans who make the *umas* report that *relicarios* are an essential ingredient in the headdresses. In 1992, New Mexican researchers Enrique de la Madrid and Barbara Mauldin examined numerous headdresses and interviewed various artisans in the province of Cotopaxi who make these elaborate costumes and rent them to festival participants. Recently made *umas*, as well as those dating to the early to mid-nineteenth century, invariably contained multiple *relicarios*; often a large *relicario* was centered at the apex of the *uma*. The

20th-century Peruvian *detente* from Cusco. The figures of the *Virgen del Carmen* and the Christ Child are fashioned of cloth and embroidery on a cardboard background. 7 cm high. Jonathon Williams Collection, Austin, Texas. Photo: AR.

Three contemporary *detentes* from Lima, Peru. Religious prints embellished with embroidery and ribbon. The largest is 5 cm. Courtesy Pachamama, Santa Fe, New Mexico. Photo: AR.

older headdresses contained *relicarios* that appeared to be bas-relief medallions sculpted of a white material, possibly a native alabaster, and framed in silver. In more recently made headdresses, the *relicarios* contained paper and cloth imagery and were framed in base metal. The artisans reported that it is now very difficult to find *relicarios* and that they search for them in the junk stores, antique shops, and markets of Ecuador and Colombia. One headdress maker showed a headdress that contained a *relicario* that he himself had fashioned: it consisted of a store-bought image of Christ, possibly in plastic, that was protected behind a round of glass that the artisan had cut from the bottom of a bottle (Mauldin 1992).

In Latacunga, Cotopaxi province, *relicarios* are also part of the *huacos*' (shamans') costumes used in the Mama Negra festival, celebrated on September 23 and 24 and again on November 11 (Naranjo 1983, 121).

In Mexico, *relicarios* are also used as symbolical and decorative elements in the dance costumes of certain Indian masked festivals. In the state of Puebla, for example, *relicarios* are part of the costumes for the Dance of the Moors and Christians, the *Danza de las Plumas* (the Dance of the Feathers), and the Battle of Puebla as seen during Carnival in the town of Huejotzingo.

In Cusco, large *relicario*-like badges with saints' pictures on them are worn by participants in processions for Corpus Christi and other festivals. These medallions, which in modern times consist of the print of a saint pasted onto cardboard and framed with an embroidered edge, are produced by nuns in a cloistered convent in Cusco; however, they are considered *detentes* by some rather than *relicarios*.

Detentes, as discussed earlier, are a type of small cloth badge or scapular found in the Andes that, like *relicarios*, have their origins in Iberian folk customs. Most typically these amulets consist of an image of the heart of Jesus, a saint, or the Virgin in cloth or paper with an embroidered edge. They are worn to protect the wearer from danger or attack. The words *detente, bala* ("stop, bullet") may appear on the badge. The wearing of *detentes* was especially popular among Carlist soldiers during nineteenth-century civil wars in Spain as well as during the Spanish Civil War of 1936–1939.

In the Andes the term *detente* as used currently refers to simple oval- and heart-shaped religious prints with embroidered edges and a ribbon loop at the top for suspension. In Colombia, heart-shaped or rectangular *detentes* are worn or hung on household walls to protect the home and its inhabitants. Sometimes the amulets are inscribed *detente—el sagrado corazón de Jesús está con migo* ("stop—the sacred heart of Jesus is with me"). In Latin America the term *detente* is also used colloquially to refer to badges worn by members of *cofradías*. In Lima, for example, pious women belonging to the Beaterio de Nazarenas wear on their traditional long purple robes *detentes* that contain an image of their patron, El Señor de los Milagros. This use appears to date back to the organization's founding in Callao in the late seventeenth century by Antonia Lucía Maldonado y Verdugo (Castañeda León 1981, 57).

18th-century Ecuadoran *detente*, silk- and metallic-thread embroidery on brocade. The legend "Halt, the heart of Jesus is with me" encircles the Central figure of Christ, fashioned in tagua nut and embroidery. 9 × 7 cm. Oswaldo Viteri Collection, Quito. Photo: CH.

18th-century Portuguese *relicario*. Bas-relief carved whalebone medallion is set into silver frame, 7 × 5.7 × 1.6 cm. Obverse: *A Virgem da Candelaria*; reverse: *São José*. Private collection. Photo: AR.

7 LUSO-BRAZILIAN *RELICARIO* TRADITIONS

IN THE FIFTEENTH CENtury, Portugal, with a population of only one and a half million, was the world's leading sea power, trading with Africa, India, the Far East, and Brazil. The riches flowing into the tiny country fueled an extraordinary expansion in the development of the arts. Architecture, painting, and sculpture during this, the Manuelian age, reflected an exuberance never again equaled in Portuguese history. Manuelian style was a triple marriage of Portugal's European Romanesque-Gothic inheritance, the Mozarabic influences of centuries of Arab occupation, and Oriental artistic traditions coming primarily from Portugal's colonies on the Indian peninsula. But the flowering of Portuguese culture was short-lived. The Spanish rule from 1580 to 1640 had a deleterious effect on the country, its arts, and the development of its largest overseas colony, Brazil.

The *relicario* traditions in Spain and her colonies were replicated in Portugal and in her New World colony, Brazil. While the information on this tradition is even more scant and difficult to find for Portugal and Brazil than for Hispanic countries, the existence of fine examples of *relicario* work in both countries, the occasional painting of a woman wearing a *relicario*, and extant inventories, wills, and other period documents attest to *relicario* traditions in Portugal and her colonies as well.

In 1609, a royal *pragmática* required the listing of all jewelry in the Portuguese city of Oporto and its environs. A number of religious jewels were owned by Francisco de Castro of the Rua de Belmonte: "a *relicario* made of enamelled gold, that has on one side Our crucified Saviour and Our Lady and Saint John, and on the other some enamel work and in the center a heart made of iridium (De Castro Pires de Lima 1960, 225)."

Because the Portuguese *relicarios* that have survived are unsigned, we can only assume that they were produced, as was much Portuguese art, by anonymous artists working for personal patrons. Portugal did produce at least two noteworthy miniaturists during the colonial period—Francisco de Holanda, 1517–1584, an outstanding illuminator trained in Michelangelo's Italy (Kubler and Soria 1959, 341), whose father, Antônio de Holanda, was also a noted miniaturist and illuminator (De Pamplona 1987, 118); and Josefa de Ayala or de Obidos, 1634?–1684 (De Pamplona 1987, 225), a devoutly religious painter, trained as an etcher, who is most well known for her finely detailed, colorful small religious scenes on copper (Kubler and Soria 1959, 343).

For a number of reasons, the arts in Portugal's only American colony never rivaled those of Spain's colonies. Brazilian painting was even less inspired than that produced in the Hispanic Americas. It, too, was almost exclusively religious, dependent upon European engravings, and almost completely devoid of local context. Martín Soria considers painting of the colonial-period in Brazil to be of "deplorable" quality (Kubler and Soria 1959, 348).

In nineteenth-century Brazil, a number of miniature portrait painters were actively producing religious miniatures for use as *relicarios*, as were many of their colleagues in the Spanish Americas.

Unlike painting, sculpture and metalwork were often of very high quality in colonial Brazil. Finely carved religious images—*santos*—and the work of Brazilian gold- and silversmiths were produced first and foremost for the church. The owners of sugar plantations and mines were also important customers, as were wealthy colonists in Spain's Río de la Plata colony to the south. Religious imagery and worked gold and silver were important mediums of exchange in the active contraband trade between the Spanish colonies and Brazil. Brazilian artisans exchanged their sculptures and silverwork for raw materials such as gold and silver (Bardi 1979, 34).

In Brazil, fine colonial-period reliquaries, large ecclesiastical objects, and small *relicarios* for private devotion can be seen in churches, museums, and private collections. In the Museum of Sacred Art in São Salvador de Bahia, for example, there are a number of large church-style reliquaries in gold and silver, as well as a gilded wood reliquary bust by Brazil's most famous sculptor of the colonial period, Antônio Francisco Lisboa (1730–1840), known affectionately as *O Aleijadinho*, "the little cripple." Fray Agostinho da Piedade, a priest and sculptor born in Portugal toward the end of the sixteenth century, created at least two reliquary busts for the Monastery of São Bento in Bahia, sometime between 1630 and 1640 (Lemos et al. 1983, 50). One, a bust of Santa Margarida, was sculpted of *barro cozido*, or baked clay, and measured 53 cm in height.

Small devotional art was originally imported from Europe into Brazil. Diminutive seventeenth- and eighteenth-century Spanish carvings in a clear colored wood not native to Brazil have been found in São Paulo (Etzel 1979, 41). Some religious ivories, probably from Goa, appeared in colonial Brazil from the seventeenth century onward. Although ivory was quite rare, Salvador was on the maritime route and ships sailing to and from the Orient called at her port. Private and museum collections of religious art in Bahia have hundreds of works of sacred art in ivory, including *relicario* images. Most Brazilian ivories are in natural white but others have been polychromed and gilded (Etzel 1979, 114).

By the second half of the eighteenth century, the combination of great distances between settlements in colonial Brazil and the "superstitious religiosity of an uncultured people (Etzel 1979, 42)" led to the rise of a number of self-taught anonymous folk sculptors producing religious imagery for popular consumption, especially in the northern states of Pernambuco and Bahia. Into the twentieth century, religious imagery, including *relicarios*, was produced by these folk artists in a variety of materials: soapstone—Minas Gerais, Bahia; bamboo shaft and *ate arame* (cooked dough)—Valley of Paraíba; ivory—São Salvador de Bahia; pine knot—São Paulo; *gesso ôco* (cast plaster)—São Paulo area, especially the pilgrimage center of Aparecida; wood—Bahia, Recife; and *osso de boi* (ox tibia)—São Paulo, Bahia. Religious folk art continues to be produced in the impoverished and isolated regions of Brazil and is especially associated with popular pilgrimage sites.

In northeastern Brazil, a common use for *relicarios* was as components in the Bahian women's *balangandãs* or *pencas*, clusters of silver charms, coins, and devotional objects worn at the waist by black slave women and, later, by Bahian market women. In a systematic study of the components of twenty-seven antique and contemporary *pencas* gathered from museums and private collections in Brazil, thirteen included *relicarios* as pendants. Most of these small silver capsules had been sealed; a few, however, displayed what appeared to be relics (Lody 1988, 155). *Relicarios* were described as being votive objects of daily use by Afro-Catholics (Lody 1988, 150).

18th-century Ecuadoran *relicario*, carved and polychromed ivory with colored-paper decorations, in gold frame approximately 6 cm in diameter. Obverse: *La Virgen Inmaculada*; reverse (not shown): *La Virgen de la Merced*. Museo Municipal Alberto Mena Caamaño, Ecuador. Photo: CH.

Late 17th-early–18th-century Philippine *relicario*. Oil on copper painting of St. Francis Xavier preaching to *indios* (Philippine natives). Reverse: numerous relics in cloth and metallic thread compartments. The case is of 20–22 k. gold, 7.2 cm in height. Jaime C. Laya Collection, Manila. Photo courtesy RV.

RELICARIO TRADITIONS
IN THE PHILIPPINES

HROUGHOUT THE LONG CO-
lonial era, the history of material culture in the Hispanic colonies of the
Americas is intertwined with that of
the Philippines. From 1570 to 1821,
when Mexico became independent from Spain, the Philippines were
administered from Mexico City, the seat of the Viceroyalty of New
Spain. Furthermore, for two hundred fifty years, beginning in 1565,
the galleon trade between Acapulco and Manila united the three con-
tinents of Asia, America, and Europe and exerted a major influence
on the decorative arts in Spain's American colonies (Martínez del Río
de Redo 1988, 70). Manila was Asia's door to the Americas.

Devotional jewelry, the vogue on the Iberian peninsula as well as
in the Americas during the colonial period, was popular and fashion-
able in the Philippines among all social classes. The Spanish historian
Delgado, writing in the mid-eighteenth century, described the Filipina women's devotional jewelry: "The Filipina women always wear
scapulars about the neck and usually some sort of small cross; and a
reliquary, containing the bones of a saint and a bit of the wood of the
cross. But this has become a part of the dress, like earrings and necklaces, and both the devout women and those who are not devout wear
them (Villegas 1983, 120)." These religious mementoes were also
thought to have protective and medicinal properties. Such beliefs have
persisted into modern times.

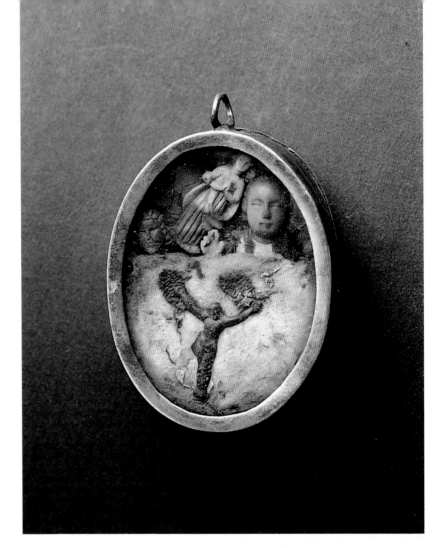

19th-century Philippine *anting-anting* (amulet) *relicario*. Various religious souvenirs with clippings from *novenarios* in a silver case, 6.2 cm in height. Southern Luzon. Ramón Villegas Collection, Manila. Photo courtesy RV.

Ramón Villegas, who has studied Philippine jewelry extensively, explains the role of jewelry based on religious imagery: "The veneration of images became a way of life, reflected in devotional jewelry. To the Filipino Christian it was an act of faith to wear them (Villegas 1983, 119)." Villegas also explains that it was an act of piety for a Christian *platero* (jeweler) to craft such work, although this was not the only consideration (Villegas 1983, 119).

Philippine *relicarios* were both simple and elegant. The most common *relicarios* were simple cases of brass or silver that contained relics labeled with the names of the saints and surrounded by sequins and gold thread—the same type of *relicario* that was popular through-out the Mediterranean and Latin America into the twentieth century.

For wealthy clients, Philippine *plateros* crafted elegant *relicario* lockets of chased gold to encase tiny religious imagery exquisitely carved in ivory by master Chinese and Filipino craftsmen. Ivory *relicario* images, whether tiny sculptures of the saints or bas-relief medallions with religious imagery, were made for home consumption as well as for export to Europe and the Americas. Villegas divides Philippine *relicario* lockets into four types: *Miniaturas*—encased paintings on ivory, canvas, board, metal; *Santos*—encased figures of ivory, gold, silver, wood; *Reliquias*—encased relics, paschal candle wax (Agnus Dei), prayer book (*devocionario*) clippings; and *tamborin* pendants, where the case, not the contents, is given greatest emphasis (Villegas 1992).

Relicarios and Agnus Dei were worn by themselves on chains or ribbons or used as pendants in elegant gold and coral *rosarios* (rosary necklaces) that were worn as devotional jewelry.

In the Philippines, the painting of *relicario* images was especially popular in the nineteenth century. Miniature portraits of the Virgin and the saints were painted in tempera on thin discs of ivory and encased in lockets of *tumbaga*, a low-karat gold alloyed with copper. These *relicarios* were hung on young girls to encourage them to be virtuous and chaste (Villegas 1983, 120).

In the nineteenth century, such artists as Damián Domingo, Hilarion Soriano, and the Asuncións, working in Manila and Laguna, painted fine religious miniatures. In the late nineteenth century, there was also a fashion of porcelain and enameled religious miniatures framed in lockets of gold and seed pearls (Villegas 1983, 120).

Damián Domingo was perhaps the finest *relicario* painter in the Philippines. Son of a Filipina mother and a Spanish father, Domingo is thought to have been born toward the end of the eighteenth century near Manila, where he died in the early 1830s (Quirino 1961, 79, 85). In 1826 this fine painter of religious subjects and portraits, especially portrait miniatures, was named director of the first Academy of Drawing in the Philippines, founded by the Economic Society of Manila in 1821 (Quirino 1961, 82). In addition to painting *relicarios*, Domingo

Early 19th-century *tamborin* necklace in 18 k. gold with *miniatura* of the *Santo Niño Dormido*, 2 cm high, carved in ivory. The necklace, of gold filigree and ivory beads, is 43 cm long. Vigan, Ilocos Sur Province, northern Luzon, Philippines. Ramón Villegas Collection, Manila. Photo courtesy RV.

Mestizo de Manila. Costumbrista watercolor by Philippine artist Damian Domingo, c. 1830, from his portfolio *Colección de Trages de Manila Tanto Antiguos como Modernos de Toda Clase de Indias*. The *mestizo* gentleman depicted is wearing a *relicario*. Photo courtesy of the Edward E. Ayer Collection, The Newberry Library, Chicago.

painted *costumbrista* portraits that often show Philippine natives wearing *relicarios*, scapulars, and other types of devotional jewelry. About 1830, only a few years prior to his death, Domingo painted a series of watercolors of these finely detailed illustrations of costumes worn by the inhabitants of Manila. Three sets of these *costumbrista* paintings are thought to exist: two in private collections in the Philippines and a third in the Newberry Library in Chicago.

By the early nineteenth century, when the Age of Reason's secularism influenced Philippine life, as it did life elsewhere in the Spanish colonies, women began to wear religious jewelry more for adornment than for devotional purposes. The *relicario* became yet another vestige of a vanished era.

GLOSSARY

AGNUS DEI: (Latin, meaning "Lamb of God") A struck-medal or wax roundel from 1 to 20 cm in diameter stamped with the Lamb of God image that signifies Christ, the sacrificial lamb. The wax Agnus is most typically fashioned from paschal candles and issued by a pope in the first year of his reign and every seven years thereafter. The reverse of the Agnus is stamped with the pope's coat of arms, images of saints to whom he is personally devoted, and the year of issuance. From the late Middle Ages on, the term "Agnus Dei" referred to a type of devotional jewel or *relicario* containing a wax Agnus. Colloquially, the term refers to a variety of devotional lockets or religious badges that may not actually contain a wax Agnus.

AUTÉNTICA: (Spanish) Certificate attesting to the authenticity of a relic or relic-bearing item such as a *relicario*, which is usually written in Latin and dated and signed by the issuing ecclesiastical authority. Often included in the sale of a *relicario* that contains actual relics.

BULLA: (Latin) In Etruscan and later Roman times, a small container, usually lenticular, made of gold or leather, meant to be suspended from a string and worn around the neck of a child as an amulet.

COFRADÍA: (Spanish) A religious society, sisterhood, or brotherhood of persons devoted in common to a holy image or purpose.

COSTUMBRISTA: (Spanish) A style of writing or painting that describes the customs popular in a particular country. In Latin America and the Philippines, a type of painting popular between the second half of the eighteenth century and the mid-nineteenth century that shows natives in traditional dress in stereotypical scenes that sometimes include local flora, fauna, and landscapes.

DETENTE: (Spanish) A type of small paper or cloth badge worn by Catholics in nineteenth- and twentieth-century Spanish-speaking countries to protect them from danger or attack. The image of the heart of Christ or Mary, or a saint's picture, is encircled with an embroidered edge. The term *detente* literally means "halt" and is directed at the devil, who is thought to be deterred at the sight of a devotee wearing this badge. *Detentes* inscribed with the words *detente bala* ("stop, bullet") were especially popular among Carlist soldiers during Spain's nineteenth-century civil wars.

ENCOLPIUM: (Latin); ENKOLPION: (Greek) An early Christian rock-crystal or glass container suspended around the neck that contained sacred mementos of the martyrs. Between the third and seventh centuries the term referred to a type of lenticular medallion or circular pendant in metal or clay that depicted in repoussé a biblical scene or the portrait of an emperor. Sometimes a cavity within provided for the safekeeping of a relic.

ESCUDO DE MONJA: (Spanish, meaning "nun's coat of arms") A type of circular or oval hagiographic badge, usually 15 to 20 cm in diameter, embroidered or painted on metal, framed in tortoiseshell, metal, or wood, worn by nuns from the seventeenth to the nineteenth century in New Spain. Especially popular with Conceptionist and Jeronymite nuns, the *escudos* bore the images of a nun's personal devotion, her name saints, or the name saints of members of her family. Also called *medallones* or *placas*.

ESTAMPA: (Spanish) A "stamp" bearing the image of a saint. In Latin America the term is used colloquially to refer to any print, usually colored, of religious subject matter.

FILACTERIA: (Spanish) Inscription on paper, parchment, ribbon, or other material that identifies the saint whose relics are contained in a *relicario*. The writing generally surrounds the relic itself or is in proximity to it.

LATITA: (Spanish) In Bolivia, a painting on a sheet of tin, most commonly of a religious subject. A popular style of religious folk art during the nineteenth century, analogous to the tin *retablo* paintings of Mexico of the same period.

LIGNUM CRUCIS: (Latin) A fragment of wood from the "true cross" of Jesus Christ, treasured as a relic throughout the Christian world from the time of Saint Helen's alleged discovery of Christ's cross in A.D. 325.

MESTIZO/A: (Spanish) A person of mixed races. In Latin America, especially one of Spanish and Indian heritages.

PLATERO/A: (Spanish) A person who works silver or gold or one who deals in such objects.

QUINTO/A: (Spanish) The fifth part. During the Spanish colonial period in Latin America, the "royal fifth" was a crown tax applied to transactions involving precious metals.

RELICARIO: (Spanish or Portuguese) Container for the safekeeping of relics. In the Americas and the Philippines the term is used colloquially to refer to lockets containing sacred imagery, relics of the saints, and personal mementos. The locket generally consists of a circular, square, oval, or hexagonal frame generally smaller than 10 cm in diameter, in silver, gold, or mixed metal with a ring at the top for suspension. The imagery within is safeguarded behind glass that affords viewing of one or both sides of the locket. In the Andes, *relicarios* are sometimes simply called *medallones*—medallions—while in Mesoamerica the term *guardapelos*—a locket specifically for the safekeeping of a lock of hair—is often used interchangeably with *relicario*.

RELIQUARY: A repository or container for relics. In medieval Europe these were often large, elaborately crafted shrines or caskets housed in churches and pilgrimage sites. Beginning in the Middle Ages in Europe, small personal reliquaries were sometimes worn by religious persons as amulets and as devotional jewelry.

ROSARIO: (Spanish or Portuguese) A style of necklace based loosely on the configuration of a Catholic rosary. Popular throughout Latin America and the Philippines, *rosarios* combine beads of gold, silver, coral, jet, wood, clay, or trade glass with religious medals, crosses, coins, amulets, charms, *relicarios*, and other items of personal significance to the wearer.

SANTO/A: (Spanish or Portuguese) A three-dimensional figure fashioned in wood, stone, clay, plaster, cloth, or other material that represents a saint of the Catholic church.

SCAPULAR: Small square of cloth, containing religious imagery, usually worn in pairs connected with ribbons, with one over the chest and another over the back. Worn by Catholics for devotional purposes and as amulets.

BIBLIOGRAPHY

Ades, Dawn. *Art in Latin America: The Modern Era 1820–1980*. New Haven and London: Yale University Press, 1989.

Ahlborn, Richard Eighme. "The Will of a New Mexico Woman in 1762." *New Mexico Historical Review* (July 1990).

Angulo Íñiguez, Diego. *Historia del Arte Hispanoamericano*. Barcelona: Salvat Editores, 1950.

Bantel, Linda, and Marcus Burke. *Spain and New Spain: Mexican Colonial Arts in Their European Context*. Corpus Christi: Art Museum of South Texas, 1979.

Barba de Piña Chan, Beatriz. "Alhajas Mexicanas." *Revista Artes de México* 165 (1960).

Bardi, Pietro María. *Arte da Prata no Brasil*. São Paulo: Banco Sudameris Brasil, 1979.

Batchen, Lou Sage. "Los Pedlars." *W. P. A. Publication 5-5-49* 50 (April 23, 1941).

Bayon, Damian, and Murillo Marx. *South American Colonial Art and Architecture*. New York: Rizzoli International, 1992.

Bentley, James. *Restless Bones: The Story of Relics*. London: Constable and Co., 1985.

Braun, Joseph. *Die Reliquiare des Christlichen Kultes und ihre Entwicklung*. Freiburg im Breisgau: Herder and Co., GMBH, 1940.

Bullock, William. *Six Months Residence and Travels in Mexico*. London: J. Murray Press, 1825.

Calderón de la Barca, Fannie Inglis. *Life in Mexico.* New York: E. P. Dutton and Co., 1931.

Carrasco Vargas, Ramón. *Arqueología y Arquitectura en el Ex-Convento de San Jerónimo.* México, D.F.: Instituto Nacional de Antropología e Historia, 1990.

Carrillo y Gariel, Abelardo. *El Traje en la Nueva España.* México, D.F.: Instituto Nacional de Antropología e Historia, 1959.

Castañeda León, Luisa. *Vestido Tradicional del Perú.* Lima: Instituto Nacional de Cultura, 1981.

Catálogo de la Colección de Relicarios. Madrid: Museo del Pueblo Español, 1952.

Chacón Torres, Mario. *Arte Virreinal en Potosí.* Sevilla: La Escuela de Estudios Hispano-Americanos de Sevilla, 1973.

Charpenel, Mauricio. *Miniaturas en el Arte Popular Mexicano.* Austin: University of Texas Press, 1970.

Ciancas, María Ester, and Barbara Meyer. *Catálogo de la Colección de Miniaturas del Museo Nacional de Historia.* México, D.F.: Instituto Nacional de Antropología e Historia, 1988.

Cobo, Bernabé. *Inca Religion and Custom.* Austin: University of Texas Press, 1990.

Cordry, Donald, and Dorothy Cordry. *Mexican Indian Costumes.* Austin: University of Texas Press, 1978.

Cornejo Bouronde, Jorge. *Derroteras de Arte Cuzqueña.* Cusco: Ediciones Inca, 1960.

Cortés, Hernán. *Cartas de Relación.* México, D.F.: Editorial Porrúa, 1988.

Cossio del Pomar, Felipe. *Arte del Perú Colonial.* México, D.F.: Fondo de Cultura Económica, 1958.

————. *Pintura Colonial (Escuela Cuzqueña).* Paris: Crete Impresor, 1929.

Coulson, John. *Dictionnaire Historique des Saints.* Paris: SEDE, 1964.

Cruz de Amenabar, Isabel. *Arte y Sociedad en Chile 1550–1650.* Santiago: Ediciones Universidad Católica de Chile, 1986.

Cuellar, Elizabeth, and Pilar Cordero. Personal correspondence, 1992.

Davis, Mary, and Greta Peck. *Mexican Jewelry.* Austin: University of Texas Press, 1963.

Dean, Carolyn Sue. "Painted Images of Cuzco's Corpus Christi: Social Conflict and Cultural Strategy in Viceregal Peru." Ann Arbor: UMI, 1990.

De Azevedo, Fernando. *Brazilian Culture.* New York: Macmillan, 1950.

De Castro Pires de Lima, Fernando. *A Arte Popular em Portugal*. Lisboa: Editorial Verbo, 1960.

De Córdova Salinas, Fray Diego, O. F. M. *Crónica Franciscana de las Provincias del Perú*. México, D.F.: Editorial Jus, 1957.

De Egaña, Antonio. *Historia de la Iglesia en la América Latina*. Madrid: Biblioteca de Autores Cristianos, 1966.

De Espinosa, Fray Isidro Félix. *Crónica de los Colegios de Propaganda Fide de la Nueva España*. Washington, D.C.: Academy of Franciscan History, 1964.

De la Cruz, Sor Juana Inés. *Obras Completas*. México, D.F.: Editorial Porrúa, 1989.

De la Maza, Francisco. *El Alabastro en el Arte Colonial de México*. México, D.F.: Instituto Nacional de Arte e Historia, 1966.

De Lavalle, José Antonio y Werner Lang. *Arte Popular: La Talla Popular en Piedra de Huamanga*. Lima: Banco de Crédito del Perú, 1980.

————. *Arte y Tesoros del Perú: Pintura Virreynal*. Lima: Banco de Crédito del Perú, 1973.

————. *Arte y Tesoros del Perú: Platería Virreynal*. Lima: Banco de Crédito del Perú, 1974.

De la Vega, Garcilaso. *Comentarios Reales: El Origen de los Incas*. Barcelona: Editorial Bruguera, 1968.

De Liébana, Joseph. "Entrega que hace el padre visitador general Manuel de Aguirre al padre Joseph de Liébana de la misión de San Luis Gonzaga de Bacadehuachi, y sus dos pueblos de visita de Nuestra Señora de Guadalupe de Nacori y San Ignacio de Mochopa el 23 de agosto de 1766." Austin: University of Texas Press, INAH, Latin American Collection, University Library, WBS 1744, Original, 455–462. At ¾ reel of Film 13.

Del Paso, Fernando. *Noticias del Imperio*. México, D.F.: Diana Literaria, 1987.

De Mesa, José. "La Pintura Cuzqueña." Madrid: Cuadernos de Arte Colonial, Museo de América, May 1988.

De Mesa, José, and Teresa Gisbert. *Historia de la Pintura Cuzqueña*. Buenos Aires: Instituto de Arte Americano e Investigaciones Estéticas, 1962.

————. *Holguín y la Pintura Virreinal en Bolivia*. La Paz: Librería Editorial la Juventud, 1977.

————. "Pintura Sobre Lata Siglo XIX." La Paz: Instituto Boliviano de Cultura, 1990.

De Pamplona, Fernando. *Diccionario de Pintores e Escultores Portugueses*. Lisboa: Livraria Civilizaçao Editora, 1987.

De Valle Arizpe, Artemio. *Notas de Platería*. México, D.F.: Herrero Hermanos, Sucesores, 1961.

Díaz del Castillo, Bernal. *Historia Verdadera de la Conquista de la Nueva España*. México, D.F.: Editorial Porrúa, S. A., 1955.

Diccionario Enciclopédico Hispano Americano. Barcelona: Monatañer y Simón, 1887.

Doelger, Franz Joseph. *Antike und Christentum*. Muenster Westfalen: Verlag Aschendorff, 1975.

Domínguez, Fray Francisco Atanasio. *The Missions of New Mexico, 1776*. Albuquerque: University of New Mexico Press, 1956.

Domínguez Bordona, Jesús. *El Arte de la Miniatura Española*. Madrid: Editorial Plutarco, 1932.

Duarte, Carlos F. *El Arte de la Platería en Venezuela*. Caracas: Fundación Pampero, 1988.

———. *Historia de la Orfebrería en Venezuela*. Caracas: Monte Avila Editores, 1970.

———. *Historia del Traje Durante la Época Colonial Venezolana*. Caracas: Gráficas Armitano, 1984.

Durandus, William. *The Symbolism of Churches*. London: Gibbings and Co., 1893.

Emmerich, André. *Sweat of the Sun and Tears of the Moon*. New York: Hacker Art Books, 1984.

Enciclopedia Universal Ilustrado. Madrid: Espas-Calpe, S.A., 1923.

Etzel, Eduardo. *Imagem Sacra Brasileira*. São Paulo: Editora da Universidade de São Paulo, 1979.

Evans, Joan. *A History of Jewellery 1100–1870*. New York: Dover Press, 1989.

Foster, George M. *Culture and Conquest: America's Spanish Heritage*. New York: Wenner-Gren Foundation for Anthropological Research, 1960.

Furlong, Guillermo. *Historia Social y Cultural del Río de la Plata*. Buenos Aires: Tipográfica Editora Argentina, 1969.

Gage, Thomas. *A New Survey of the West Indies*. London: R. Cotes, 1648.

Gatbonton, Esperanza Bunag. *Carvings in Ivory*. Manila: Intramuros Administration, 1983.

———. *A Heritage of Saints: Colonial Santos in the Philippines*. Manila: Editorial Associates, 1979.

Giffords, Gloria Kay. *Mexican Folk Retablos: Masterpieces on Tin*. Tucson: University of Arizona Press, 1974.

Giraldo Jaramillo, Gabriel. *La Miniatura, la Pintura y el Grabado en Colombia*. Bogotá: Gráfica Cabrera e Hijos, 1982.

———. *Notas y Documentos Sobre el Arte en Colombia*. Bogotá: Editorial ABC, 1954.

———. *La Pintura en Colombia*. México, D.F.: Fondo de Cultura Económica, 1948.

Gisbert, Teresa. "Arte Boliviano del Siglo XIX." La Paz: Encuentro, Revista Boliviana de Cultura, Diciembre, 1990.

———. *Iconografía y Mitos Indígenas en el Arte*. La Paz: Editorial Gisbert y Cía, S.A., 1980.

———. "La Pintura en Potosí y la Audiencia de Charcas." Madrid: Cuadernos de Arte Colonial, Museo de América, Octubre 1987.

Gloria in Excelsis: The Virgin and Angels in Viceregal Painting of Peru and Bolivia. New York: Catalogue of the Center for Inter-American Relations, 1985.

Gold and Silver of the Atocha and Santa Margarita. New York: Christie's, auction catalogue, June 14–15, 1988.

Gómez-Tabanera, José Manuel. *Trajes Populares y Costumbres Tradicionales*. Madrid: Editorial Tesoro, Ediciones Siglo XX, 1950.

González Obregón, Luis. *Croniquillas de la Nueva España*. México, D.F.: Ediciones Bota, 1936.

Granados, María Josefa. "Original Procedimiento Judicial del Último Testamento e Inventario." Bexar County Archive, Wills and Estates, vol. 2, no. 9, San Antonio, Texas, 1787.

Hammond, George, and Agapito Rey. *Oñate, Colonizer of New Mexico 1595–1628*. Albuquerque: University of New Mexico Press, 1953.

Hassan de Llorente, Carmen. *La Orfebrería Popular de Panamá*. Panamá: Instituto Nacional de Cultura, 1983.

Historia de Arte Mexicano, Volumen VI. México, D.F.: Salvat Mexicano de Ediciones, 1982.

Hoberman, Louisa Schell, and Susan Migden Socolow, eds. *Cities and Society in Colonial Latin America*. Albuquerque: University of New Mexico Press, 1986.

The Holy Bible: Authorized King James Version. Cleveland and New York: World Publishing Co., 1950.

Hunter, R. Vernon. "Spanish Colonial Arts in New Mexico." *W.P.A. Publication 5-5-57* 2 (April 22, 1937).

Hussey, J. M. *The Byzantine World*. New York: Harper and Brothers, 1961.

Imágenes Guadalupanas Cuatro Siglos. México, D.F.: Centro Cultural Arte Contemporáneo, Fundación Cultural Televisa, 1987.

The Jewish Encyclopedia. New York: Funk and Wagnalls, 1902.

Juan, Jorge, and Antonio de Ulloa. *A Voyage to South America*. Boston: Milford House, 1972.

Keleman, Pál. *Art of the Americas: Ancient and Hispanic*. New York: Thomas Y. Crowell, 1969.

———. *Baroque and Rococo in Latin America*. New York: Macmillan, 1951.

———. *El Greco Revisited*. New York: Macmillan, 1961.

———. *Peruvian Colonial Painting*. New York: Meridan Gravure, 1971.

Kubler, George. *Santos: An Exhibition of the Religious Folk Art of New Mexico*. Fort Worth: Amon Carter Museum of Western Art, 1964.

Kubler, George, and Martín Soria. *Art and Architecture in Spain and Portugal and Their American Dominions 1500–1800*. Baltimore: Penguin Books, 1959.

Lebret, Iveline. *La Vida en Otavalo en el Siglo XVIII*. Otavalo: Editorial Gallocapitán, 1981.

Lemos, Carlos, José Roberto Teixeira Leite, and Pedro Manuel Gismonti. *The Art of Brazil*. New York: Harper and Row, 1983.

Lody, Raul. *Pencas de Balangandãs da Bahia: Um Estudo Etnográfico das Joias-amuletos*. Rio de Janeiro: Instituto Nacional do Folclore, 1988.

Lopétegui, León, S. I., and Felix Zubillaga, S. I. *Historia de la Iglesia en la América Española*. Madrid: La Editorial Católica, 1965.

López, Alfred. "The Roots of the Rose." Unpublished dissertation, University of New Mexico, Albuquerque, 1993.

Macera, Pablo. *Pintores Populares Andinos*. Lima: Fondo del Libro del Banco de los Andes, 1979.

Malkiel-Jirmounsky, Myron. *Problèmes des Primitifs Portugais*. Coimbra: Coimbra Editora, 1941.

Martínez del Río de Redo, Marita, et al. *El Galeón de Acapulco*. México, D.F.: INAH, 1988.

Mauldin, Barbara. "Corpus Christi Dance Costumes of Cotopaxi, Ecuador." Unpublished manuscript, University of New Mexico, Albuquerque, December 1992.

Mexico: Splendors of Thirty Centuries. New York: Metropolitan Museum of Art, 1990.

Mugaburu, Josephe de. *Chronicle of Colonial Lima*. Norman: University of Oklahoma Press, 1975.

Muller, Priscilla E. *Jewelry in Spain 1500–1800*. New York: Hispanic Society of America, 1972.

Muratorio, Ricardo. "A Feast of Color: Corpus Christi Dance Costumes of Ecuador." Washington, D.C.: Smithsonian Institution Press, 1981.

Muriel de la Torre, Josefina. *Conventos de Monjas en la Nueva España*. México, D.F.: Editorial Santiago, 1946.

———. "Monjas Coronadas." México, D.F.: Artes de México, 1960.

Muriel de la Torre, Josefina, and Manuel Romero de Terreros. *Retratos de Monjas*. México, D.F.: Editorial Jus, 1952.

Naranjo, Marcelo V. *La Cultura Popular en el Ecuador, Tomo II: Cotopaxi*. Cuenca: CIDAP, 1983.

New Catholic Encyclopedia, Vol. XII. New York: McGraw Hill, 1967.

Newman, Harold. *An Illustrated Dictionary of Jewellery*. London: Thames and Hudson, 1981.

Newton, A. P. *Thomas Gage, the English American: A New Survey of the West Indies, 1648*. London: Lund Humphries, 1946.

Obregón, Gonzalo. "La Colección de Miniaturas del Museo Nacional de Historia." México, D.F.: Revista Artes de México, no. 159, 1960.

Onelli, Clemente. *Hagiografía Argentina*. Buenos Aires: Imprenta Guillermo Kraft, 1916.

Ongpin, Stephen. *Damian Domingo, Filipino Master*. Manila: Intramuros Administration, 1983.

Ortiz Echagüe, José. *España, Tipos y Trajes*. Madrid: Publicaciones Ortiz Echagüe, 1917.

Otero, Gustavo Adolfo. *La Vida Social en el Coloniaje*. La Paz: Editorial Juventud, 1958.

Out of the Opulent Past: Italian Treasures from the Etruscan Age to the Renaissance. Florence: Nuova Grafica Fiorentina, 1992.

Palmer, Gabrielle. *Sculpture in the Kingdom of Quito*. Albuquerque: University of New Mexico Press, 1987.

Pereira Salas, Eugenio. *Historia del Arte en el Reino de Chile*. Santiago: Ediciones de la Universidad de Chile, 1965.

Ponce Sanginés, Carlos. *Tunupa y Ekako*. La Paz: Academia Nacional de Ciencias de Bolivia, 1969.

Prescott, William H. *History of the Conquest of Mexico*. Philadelphia: J. B. Lippincott, 1860.

Quintana, José Miguel. *Agnus Dei y Otras Noticias Relativas*. México, D.F.: Editorial Cultura, 1965.

Quirino, Carlos, F.R.G.S. "Damian Domingo, First Eminent Philippine Painter." *Philippine Studies* 9, 1 (January 1961).

Réau, Louis. *Iconografie de l'Art Chrétien*. Paris: Presses Universitaires de France, 1955.

"Le reliquaire le plus extraordinaire." Paris: Connaissance des Arts, Janvier 1967.

Rey, Agapito. *Cultura y Costumbres del Siglo XVI en la Península Ibérica y en Nueva España*. México, D.F.: Ediciones Mensaje, 1944.

Romero de Terreros, Manuel. *El Arte en México Durante el Virreinato*. México, D.F.: Editorial Porrúa, 1951.

———. *Las Artes Industriales de la Nueva España*. México, D.F.: 1923.

———. "La Casa del Conde de Xala." *Memorias de la Academia Mexicana III* 3 (julio–septiembre 1944).

———. *Miscelánea de Arte Colonial*. México, D.F.: Reaseguros Alianza, 1990.

Sánchez Herrero, José. *Las Cofradías de Sevilla*. Sevilla: La Universidad de Sevilla, 1980.

Sánchez Navarro de Pintado, Beatriz. *Marfiles Cristianos del Oriente en México*. México, D.F.: Fomento Cultural Banamex, A.C., 1985.

Sanjinés, P. Fernando de M. *Historia del Santuario e Imagen de Copacabana*. La Paz: Tipografía La Unión, 1909.

Sola, Miguel. *Historia del Arte Hispano-Americano*. Barcelona: Editorial Labor, 1935.

Solano, Francisco de. *Antonio de Ulloa y la Nueva España*. México, D.F.: Universidad Nacional Autónoma de México, 1987.

Soria, Martín S. *La Pintura del Siglo XVI en Sud América*. Buenos Aires: 1956.

Stastny, Francisco. *Breve Historia de Arte en el Perú*. Lima: Editorial Universo, 1967.

———. *Las Artes Populares del Perú*. Madrid: Alianza Editorial, 1971.

Taullard, A. *Platería Sudamericana*. Buenos Aires: Ediciones Peuser, 1947.

Toussaint, Manuel. *Arte Colonial en México*. México, D.F.: Imprenta Universitaria, 1948.

————. *Pintura Colonial en México*. México, D.F.: Imprenta Universitaria, 1965.

Tovar de Teresa, Guillermo. *Pintura y Escultura del Renacimiento en México*. México, D.F.: Instituto Nacional de Antropología e Historia, 1979.

————. *Un Rescate de la Fantasía: El Arte de los Lagarto, Iluminadores Novohispanos de los Siglos XVI y XVII*. Madrid: Ediciones del Equilibrista, 1988.

Turner, Victor, and Edith Turner. *Image and Pilgrimage in Christian Culture*. New York: Columbia University Press, 1978.

Vargas, José María, O.P. *El Arte Quiteño en los Siglos XVI, XVII, XVIII*. Quito: Litografía Imprenta Romero, 1949.

————. *La Iglesia y el Patrimonio Cultural Ecuatoriano*. Quito: Ediciones de la Universidad Católica, 1982.

Vargas Lugo, Elisa. "La Expresión Pictórica Religiosa y La Sociedad Colonial." *Anales del Instituto de Investigaciones Estéticas* 50/1 (1982).

————. *Juan Correa: Su Vida y Su Obra*. México, D.F.: UNAM, 1985.

Vargas Ugarte, Rubén, S.J. *Ensayo de un Diccionario de Artífices*. Burgos: Imprenta de Aldecoa, 1968.

————. *Historia del Culto de María en Iberoamérica y de Sus Imágenes y Santuarios Más Celebrados, Tomos I y II*. Madrid: Talleres Gráficas Jura, 1956.

Vásquez de Espinosa, Antonio. *Compendio y Descripción de las Indias Occidentales*. Madrid: Ediciones Atlas, 1969.

Velasco Ibarra, Enrique. *Monjas Coronadas*. México, D.F.: Secretaria Particular de la Presidencia, 1978.

Veyne, Paul. *Histoire de la Vie Privé: De l'Empire Romain a l'An Mil*. Paris: Editions du Seuil, 1985.

Vikan, Gary. *Byzantine Pilgrimage Art*. Washington, D.C.: Dumbarton Oaks, 1982.

Villegas, Ramón N. *Kayamanan: The Philippine Jewelry Tradition*. Manila: Central Bank of the Philippines, 1983.

————. Personal correspondence, 1992.

Von Barghan, Barbara, ed. *Temples of Gold, Crowns of Silver: Reflections of Majesty in the Viceregal Americas*. Washington, D.C.: George Washington University, 1991.

Walters Art Gallery. *Jewelry: Ancient to Modern*. New York: Viking Press, 1979.

Weckman, Luis. *La Herencia Medieval de México, Volúmenes I y II*. México, D.F.: El Colegio de México, 1984.

Weisman, Elizabeth Wilder. *Americas: The Decorative Arts in Latin America in the Era of the Revolution*. Washington, D.C.: Smithsonian Institution Press, 1976.

Williams, Leonard. *The Arts and Crafts of Older Spain*. Chicago: A. C. McClurg and Co., 1908.

Wroth, William. *Christian Images in Hispanic New Mexico*. Colorado Springs: Fine Arts Center, Taylor Museum, 1982.

INDEX